Common CORE Mathematics

Practice at 3 Levels ●●●

Table of Contents

Using This Book

What Is the Common Core?

The Common Core State Standards are an initiative by the states to set shared, consistent, and clear expectations of what students are expected to learn, so teachers and parents know what they need to do to help them. The standards are designed to be rigorous and pertinent to the real world. They reflect the knowledge and skills that our young people need for success in college and careers.

What Are the Intended Outcomes of Common Core?

The goal of the Common Core Standards is to facilitate the following competencies.

Students will:
- demonstrate independence;
- build strong content knowledge;
- respond to the varying demands of audience, task, purpose, and discipline;
- comprehend as well as critique;
- value evidence;
- use technology and digital media strategically and capably;
- come to understand other perspectives and cultures.

What Does This Mean for You?

If your state has joined the Common Core State Standards Initiative, then as a teacher you are required to incorporate these standards into your lesson plans. Your students may need targeted practice in order to meet grade-level standards and expectations and thereby be promoted to the next grade. This book is appropriate for on-grade-level students as well as intervention, ELs, struggling readers, and special needs. To see if your state has joined the initiative, visit the Common Core States Standards Initiative website to view the most recent adoption map: http://www.corestandards.org/in-the-states.

What Does the Common Core Say Specifically About Math?

For math, the Common Core sets the following key expectations.

- Make sense of problems and persevere in solving them.
- Reason abstractly and quantitatively.
- Construct viable arguments and critique the reasoning of others.
- Model with mathematics.
- Use appropriate tools strategically.
- Attend to precision.
- Look for and make use of structure.
- Look for and express regularity in repeated reasoning.

Common Core Mathematics Grade 1 • ©2012 Newmark Learning, LLC

How Does Common Core Mathematics Help My Students?

- **Mini-lesson for each unit** introduces
  Common Core math skills and concepts.

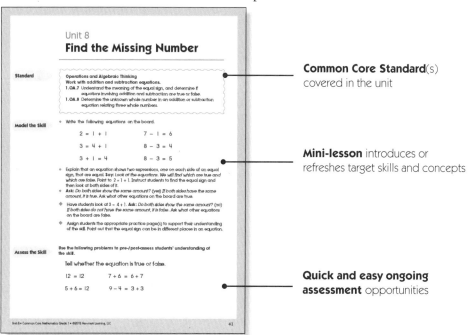

Common Core Standard(s)
covered in the unit

Mini-lesson introduces or
refreshes target skills and concepts

**Quick and easy ongoing
assessment** opportunities

- **Four practice pages** with three levels of differentiated practice,
  and word problems follow each mini-lesson.

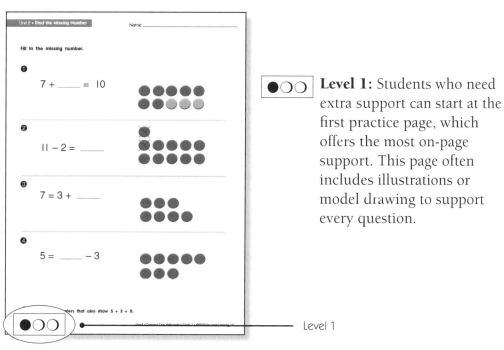

Level 1: Students who need
extra support can start at the
first practice page, which
offers the most on-page
support. This page often
includes illustrations or
model drawing to support
every question.

Level 1

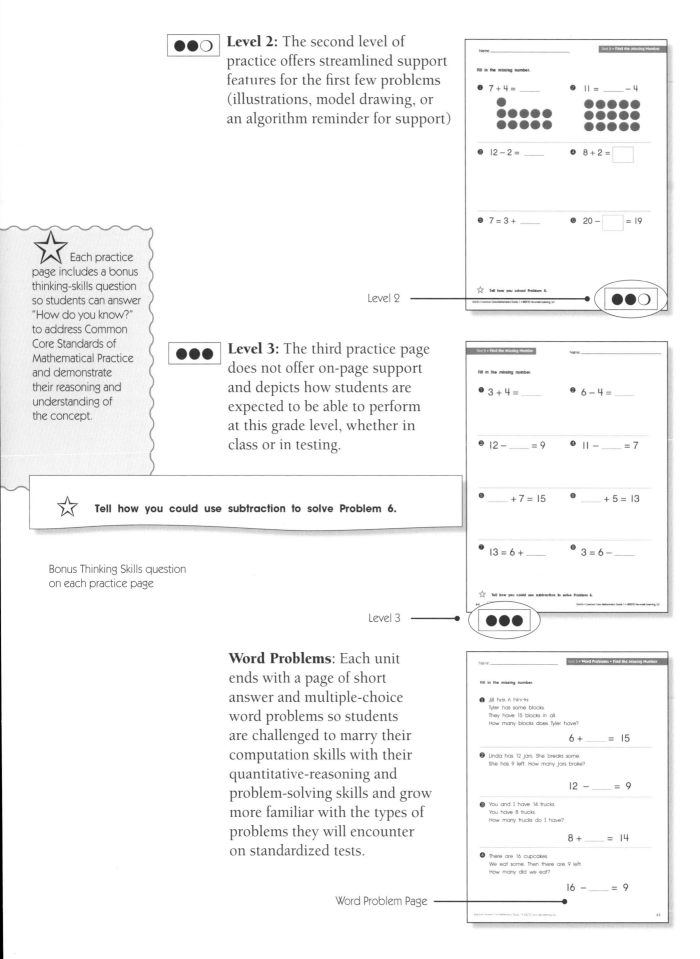

Level 2: The second level of practice offers streamlined support features for the first few problems (illustrations, model drawing, or an algorithm reminder for support)

☆ Each practice page includes a bonus thinking-skills question so students can answer "How do you know?" to address Common Core Standards of Mathematical Practice and demonstrate their reasoning and understanding of the concept.

Level 2

Level 3: The third practice page does not offer on-page support and depicts how students are expected to be able to perform at this grade level, whether in class or in testing.

☆ **Tell how you could use subtraction to solve Problem 6.**

Bonus Thinking Skills question on each practice page

Level 3

Word Problems: Each unit ends with a page of short answer and multiple-choice word problems so students are challenged to marry their computation skills with their quantitative-reasoning and problem-solving skills and grow more familiar with the types of problems they will encounter on standardized tests.

Word Problem Page

Common Core Standards Alignment Chart • Grade 1

Units	1.OA.1	1.OA.2	1.OA.3	1.OA.4	1.OA.5	1.OA.6	1.OA.7	1.OA.8	1.NBT.1	1.NBT.2	1.NBT.3	1.NBT.4	1.NBT.5	1.NBT.6	1.MD.1	1.MD.2	1.MD.3	1.MD.4	1.G.1	1.G.2	1.G.3
Operations & Algebraic Thinking																					
Unit 1: Add To and Take From	✔			✔																	
Unit 2: Put Together and Take Apart	✔			✔																	
Unit 3: Add and Subtract to Compare	✔			✔																	
Unit 4: Add Three Numbers		✔																			
Unit 5: Use Properties of Addition to Add		✔	✔																		
Unit 6: Use Strategies to Add			✔		✔	✔															
Unit 7: Use Strategies to Subtract			✔	✔	✔	✔															
Unit 8: Find the Missing Number							✔	✔													
Numbers & Operations in Base Ten																					
Unit 9: Count, Read, and Write Numbers to 120									✔												
Unit 10: Tens and Ones										✔											
Unit 11: Compare Numbers										✔	✔										
Unit 12: Add Two-Digit and One-Digit Numbers												✔	✔	✔							
Unit 13: Ten More, Ten Less												✔	✔								
Unit 14: Add Multiples of Ten												✔									
Unit 15: Subtract Multiples of Ten														✔							
Measurement & Data																					
Unit 16: Compare and Order Lengths															✔	✔					
Unit 17: Measure Length with Non-Standard Units																✔					
Unit 18: Tell and Write Time																	✔				
Unit 19: Interpret Data																		✔			
Geometry																					
Unit 20: Use Plane Shapes																			✔		
Unit 21: Use Solid Shapes																				✔	
Unit 22: Parts of Shapes																					✔

Unit 1
Add To and Take From

Standard

Operations and Algebraic Thinking
Represent and solve problems involving addition and subtraction.
1.OA.1 Use addition and subtraction within 20 to solve word problems involving situations of adding to, taking from, putting together, taking apart, and comparing, with unknowns in all positions, e.g., by using objects, drawings, and equations with a symbol for the unknown number to represent the problem.

Understand and apply properties of operations and the relationship between addition and subtraction.
1.OA.4 Understand subtraction as an unknown-addend problem.

Model the Skill

◆ Hand out 20 counters and write the following word problem on the board.

5 ducks are in a pond.

Then 7 more ducks go into the pond.

How many ducks are in the pond?

◆ **Say:** *Let's read the word problem together. We will use counters to act out the problem.* Read the problem aloud.

◆ Read the first line. **Ask:** *How many ducks are in the pond?* (5) Have students use 5 counters to stand for the 5 ducks. **Ask:** *How many more ducks come?* (7) *How many more counters should you take?* (7) Have students take 7 more counters. Explain that since more came, they need to add the counters or push them together. **Ask:** *How many ducks are in the pond now?* (12)

◆ Assign students the appropriate practice page(s) to support their understanding of the skill.

Assess the Skill

Use the following problems to pre- or post-assess students' understanding of the skill.

$2 + 6 = \underline{8}$ $8 - 2 = \underline{6}$ $8 - 6 = \underline{2}$

$5 + 4 = \underline{9}$ $9 - 4 = \underline{5}$ $9 - 5 = \underline{4}$

$8 + 3 = \underline{11}$ $11 - 3 = \underline{8}$ $11 - 8 = \underline{}$

Name _____

Use to solve each problem.

counters

1 There are 3 turtles in the sand.
6 more turtles come.
How many turtles are in the sand now?

$3 + 6 = \underline{9}$ 🐢🐢
turtles

---

2 There are 12 birds in a tree.
4 birds fly away.
How many birds are left in the tree?

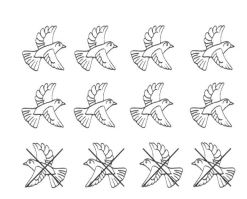

$12 - 4 = \underline{8}$ 🐦🐦
birds

---

3 There are 11 ducks in the pond.
3 ducks are brown. The others are white.
How many ducks are white?

$3 + \underline{8} = 11$ 🦆🦆
ducks

☆ **Point to the symbol that tells you when to add.**

Name _____

Use drawings to solve each problem.

1 Ted has 9 cars.

He gets 3 more cars.

How many cars does he have now?

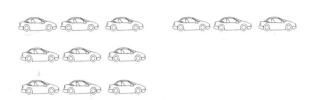

$$9 + 3 = \underline{12}$$

Ted has __12__ cars.

---

2 Riley had 4 crayons.

She finds some more crayons.

Now she has 12 crayons.

How many crayons did she find?

$$4 + \underline{8} = 12$$

Riley finds __8__ crayons.

---

3 Meg baked 6 muffins.

She ate 2 muffins.

How many muffins does she have left?

$$6 - 2 = \underline{4}$$

Meg has __4__ muffins.

 Tell how you know when to add.

●●○

Use to solve each problem.
counters

1 We had 10 dolls.
We bought 4 more.
How many dolls do we have now?

$$10 + 4 = \underline{14} \text{ dolls.}$$

2 Ann had 16 hair clips.
She lost 7 hair clips.
How many hair clips does she have now?

$$16 - 7 = \underline{9} \text{ hair clips.}$$

3 Dad baked 13 rolls.
We ate some rolls.
Then there were 8 rolls.
How many rolls did we eat?

$$13 - \underline{5} = 8 \text{ rolls.}$$

4 Mary had some balloons. Then 9 balloons popped.
She has 9 balloons left. How many balloons did
she have before?

$$\underline{18} - 9 = 9 \text{ balloons.}$$

 Tell how you solved the Problem 4.

Name _____

Solve.

1 There were 7 ducks in the pond.
Then 4 more came.
How many ducks are in the pond now?

$$7 + 4 = \underline{11} \text{ ducks}$$

2 Dad had some pencils.
Then he found 10 more pencils.
Now he has 15 pencils in all.
How many pencils did Dad
have at first?

$$\underline{5} + 10 = 15 \text{ pencils}$$

3 There were 13 marbles in the bag.
David took out 5 marbles.
How many marbles are left in the bag?

$$13 - 5 = \underline{8} \text{ marbles}$$

4 There were 4 frogs in a pond.
Some more frogs came.
Then there were 10 frogs.
How many more frogs came?

$$4 + \underline{6} = 10 \text{ frogs}$$

Unit 2
Put Together and Take Apart

Standard

Operations and Algebraic Thinking

Represent and solve problems involving addition and subtraction.

1.OA.1 Use addition and subtraction within 20 to solve word problems involving situations of adding to, taking from, putting together, taking apart, and comparing, with unknowns in all positions, e.g., by using objects, drawings, and equations with a symbol for the unknown number to represent the problem.

Understand and apply properties of operations and the relationship between addition and subtraction.

1.OA.4 Understand subtraction as an unknown-addend problem.

Model the Skill

◆ Hand out 20 counters and write the following word problem on the board.

There are 6 corn muffins and 8 blueberry muffins in the oven.

How many muffins are in the oven?

◆ **Say:** *Let's read this problem together.* Read the problem aloud. **Say:** *We will use counters to act out the problem.*

◆ Read the first line. **Ask:** *How many corn muffins are in the oven?* (6) Have students use 6 counters for the 6 corn muffins. **Ask:** *How many blueberry muffins are in the oven?* (8) Have students take 8 counters. **Ask:** *What do you have to do to find how many muffins are in the oven?* (push the counters together and count how many in all) **Ask:** *How many muffins are in the oven?* (14)

◆ Then help students write an addition sentence for the problem.

◆ Assign students the appropriate practice page(s) to support their understanding of the skill. Encourage students to check their work.

Assess the Skill

Use the following problems to pre-/post-assess students' understanding of the skill.

$4 + 3 = 7$ $7 - 3 = 4$ $7 - 4 = 3$

$4 + 6 = 10$ $10 - 4 = 6$ $10 - 6 = 4$

$8 + 5 = 13$ $12 - 5 = 7$ $12 - 7 = 5$

Name _____

Use to solve each problem.

counters

1 We have 4 yellow bananas.
We have 2 green bananas.
How many bananas do
we have in all?

$4 + 2 = \underline{6}$ bananas in all

---

2 There are 5 red cups.
There are 3 blue cups.
How many cups are there in all?

$5 + 3 = \underline{8}$ cups in all

---

3 Reed has 6 trucks.
Sara has 5 trucks.
How many trucks do they have in all?

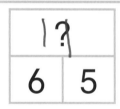

1?	
6	5

$6 + 5 = \underline{11}$ trucks in all

---

4 There are 12 muffins.
7 are blueberry. The others are corn.
How many corn muffins are there?

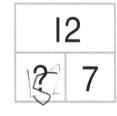

12	
5?	7

$7 + \underline{5} = 12$ $12 - 7 = \underline{5}$ corn muffins

☆ **Point to the symbol that tells you when to subtract.**

Name  Riley

For each problem, use counters to solve.

1 We have 5 red crayons.
We have 9 blue crayons.
How many crayons do we have in all?

$5 + 9 = 14$ crayons

2 14 buses are at the station.
6 buses drive away.
How many buses are left?

$14 - 6 = 8$ buses

3 The park has 12 swings.
5 swings have people.
The rest are empty.
How many swings are empty?

$5 + 7 = 12$ swings

4 Dad made 6 tacos.
He has 2 plates.
How many tacos can
Dad put on each plate?

$3 + 3 = 6$ tacos

$3 + 3 = 6$ tacos

 Tell how you solved the Problem 4.

Name _____

For each problem, use counters . Write two different ways to solve.

1 A rancher has 7 horses.
She sells some horses.
She has 2 horses left.
How many horses did she sell?

$$7 - \underline{5} = 2 \text{ horses}$$

2 A farmer has 9 pigs.
He buys 3 more pigs.
How many pigs does
he have now?

$$9 + 3 = \underline{12} \text{ pigs}$$

3 The pet store has 8 dogs.
The store has 2 cages.
How many dogs can be
in each cage?

$$\underline{4} + \underline{4} = 8 \text{ dogs}$$
$$\underline{4} + \underline{4} = 8 \text{ dogs}$$

4 The baker has 10 rolls.
He has two baskets.
How many rolls can
he put in each basket?

$$\underline{5} + \underline{5} = 10 \text{ rolls}$$
$$\underline{5} + \underline{5} = 10 \text{ rolls}$$

☆ **What is another way to solve Problem 4? Tell why.**

● ● ●

Unit 2 • Common Core Mathematics Grade 1 • ©2012 Newmark Learning, LLC

For each problem, use counters . **Write two different ways to solve.**

1 Lila has 5 plants.
She bought 7 more plants.
How many plants does she have in now?

$$5 + 7 = 12 \text{ plants}$$

2 Will buys 6 fish.
He gives some fish away.
He has 4 fish left.
How many fish did he give away?

$$6 - 2 = 4 \text{ fish}$$

3 Emma has 7 crabs
in 2 tanks. How many crabs
can she have in each tank?

$$3 + 4 = 7 \text{ crabs}$$
$$4 + 3 = 7 \text{ crabs}$$

4 Ken has 6 frogs in 2 tanks.
How many frogs can he
have in each tank?

$$3 + 3 = 6 \text{ frogs}$$
$$3 + 3 = 6 \text{ frogs}$$

Unit 3
Add and Subtract to Compare

Operations and Algebraic Thinking

Represent and solve problems involving addition and subtraction.

1.OA.1 Use addition and subtraction within 20 to solve word problems involving situations of adding to, taking from, putting together, taking apart, and comparing, with unknowns in all positions, e.g., by using objects, drawings, and equations with a symbol for the unknown number to represent the problem.

Understand and apply properties of operations and the relationship between addition and subtraction.

1.OA.4 Understand subtraction as an unknown-addend problem.

Model the Skill

◆ Hand out 20 counters and write the following word problem on the board.

Jesse has 7 stickers. Stella has 11 stickers.

How many more stickers does Stella have

compared with Jesse?

◆ **Say:** *We will use a different color counter for each child.* Have students use 7 red counters to represent Jesse's stickers and 11 yellow counters for Stella's stickers. Show them how to align the two rows to compare. **Say:** *Look at the two rows.*

◆ **Ask:** *How many more counters are in the bottom row than the top row?* (4) Help students make pairs matching the top and bottom counters. Have them count how many more are in the bottom row, or do not have a pair. **Ask:** *How many more stickers does Stella have than Jesse?* (4)

◆ Assign students the appropriate practice page(s) to support their understanding of the skill.

Assess the Skill

Use the following problems to pre-/post-assess students' understanding of the skill.

I have 8 apples.
I need 10 to make a pie.
How many more apples
do I need?

Mom has 11 paper clips.
Sam has 6 paper clips.
How many more paper clips
does Mom have than Sam?

Name _____

Use ⬤◯ counters to solve each problem.

1 Ryan has 3 stickers.
Clare has 6 stickers.
How many more stickers
does Clare have than Ryan?

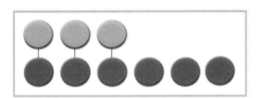

$3 + \underline{3} = 6$

Clare has _3_ more stickers.

---

2 Olivia buys 4 pencils.
Noah buys 7 pencils.
How many more pencils
does Noah buy than Olivia?

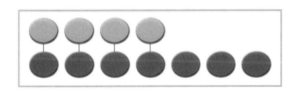

$4 + \underline{3} = 7$

Noah has _3_ more pencils.

---

3 Ray buys 12 pens.
Nick buys 5 pens.
How many more pens
does Ray buy than Nick?

$12 - 5 = \underline{7}$

Ray buys _5_ more pens.

 Circle the number that shows how many pens Nick bought.

Name _____

Use to solve each problem.

counters

1 Taylor has 2 crayons.
Kylee has 3 more crayons.
How many crayons does Kylee have?

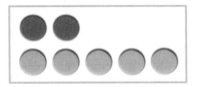

$$2 + 3 = \underline{5} \text{ crayons}$$

2 Maya finds 9 leaves.
Joe finds 4 leaves.
How many fewer leaves
does Joe find than Maya?

$$9 - 4 = \underline{5} \text{ fewer leaves}$$

3 Stella has 7 buttons.
Nico has 15 buttons.
How many fewer buttons
does Stella have than Nico?

$$15 - 7 = \underline{8} \text{ fewer buttons}$$

4 Jake has 12 flowers.
Michel has 3 flowers.
How many fewer flowers
does Michel have?

$$12 - 3 = \underline{9} \text{ fewer flowers}$$

 Tell how you know Jake has more flowers than Michel.

Name Riley

Use to solve each problem.
counters

1 Matt has 4 apples.
Riley has 3 more apples than Matt.
How many apples does Riley have?

$$4 + 3 = \underline{7} \text{ apples}$$

---

2 Lily takes 9 marbles.
Zoe takes 5 more marbles than Lily.
How many marbles does Zoe take?

$$9 + 5 = \underline{14} \text{ marbles}$$

---

3 Will has 8 goldfish.
Ella has 14 goldfish.
How many fewer goldfish
does Will have than Ella?

$$14 - 8 = \underline{6} \text{ fewer goldfish}$$

---

4 Carmen has 9 shells.
Peter has 19 shells.
How many fewer shells does
Carmen have than Peter?

$$19 - 9 = \underline{10} \text{ fewer shells}$$

 Tell how you solved Problem 4.

Name _____

Use to solve each problem.

counters

1 Tessa has 6 pears.

Drew has 3 pears.

How many fewer pears does Drew have?

$6 - 3 = \underline{3}$ Drew has _____ fewer pears.

2 Mom has 3 books.

Dad has 5 books.

How many more books does Dad have?

$3 + \underline{2} = 5$ Dad has __5__ more books.

3 Mrs. Rose has 15 stamps.

Mr. Brown has 6 fewer stamps than Mrs. Rose.

How many stamps does Mr. Brown have?

$15 - 6 = \underline{9}$ Mr. Brown has __6__ stamps.

4 Caden has 13 balloons.

Allison has 9 fewer balloons than Caden.

How many balloons does Allison have?

$13 - 9 = \underline{4}$ Allison has __9__ balloons.

Unit 4
Add Three Numbers

Standard

Operations and Algebraic Thinking
Represent and solve problems involving addition and subtraction.
1.OA.2 Solve word problems that call for addition of three whole numbers whose sum is less than or equal to 20, e.g., by using objects, drawings, and equations with a symbol for the unknown number to represent the problem.

Model the Skill

◆ Hand out 20 counters and write the following word problem on the board.

April has 4 marbles. Renee has 6 marbles and Eric has 5 marbles.

How many marbles do they have in all?

◆ **Say:** *Let's read the word problem together. We will use counters to act out the problem.* Read the problem aloud.

◆ Read the first line. **Ask:** *How many counters should you take?* (4) Have students take 4 counters to represent April's 4 marbles. Read the next line. **Ask:** *How many counters should you take for Renee's marbles?* (6) Help students take the correct number of counters. **Ask:** *How many counters should you take for Eric's marbles?* (5)

◆ **Ask:** *How many marbles are there in all?* Help students understand that they need to count all the counters to find how many in all. (15)

◆ Assign students the appropriate practice page(s) to support their understanding of the skill. Have them use counters or drawings.

Assess the Skill

Use the following problems to pre-/post-assess students' understanding of the skill.

The table has 3 blue cups,
7 yellow cups, and 6 red cups.
How many cups are on the table?

I have 6 blue folders,
5 white folders, and 8 red folders.
How many folders do I have?

Name _____

Add. Use to solve.
counters

1 There are 2 red flowers,
3 yellow flowers, and 4 orange flowers.
How many flowers are there in all?

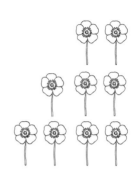

__9__ flowers

2 A pond has 4 red fish,
6 blue fish, and 2 yellow fish.
How many fish are there in all?

__12__ fish

3 8 girls get on the bus.
3 boys get on the bus.
5 more boys get on the bus.
How many children are
on the bus now?

$8 + 3 + 5 = \underline{16}$

__16__ children

 Circle the problems where you used addition.

Name _____

Add. Use counters or drawings to solve.

1 Linda has 4 jars. Todd has 6 jars.
Ryan has 3 jars.
How many jars do they have in all?

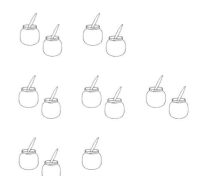

_13_ jars

2 Sue has 2 blocks. Paul has 5 blocks.
Ria has 4 blocks.
How many blocks do they have in all?

_10_ blocks

3 Liv has 2 cars. Jack has 6 cars.
Mark has 1 car.
How many cars do they have in all?

$2 + 6 + 1 =$ _9_   _9_ cars

4 There are 4 pink cupcakes.
There are 2 yellow cupcakes and 7 blue cupcakes.
How many cupcakes are there in all?

$4 + 2 + 7 =$ _13_   _12_ cupcakes

 Tell how you solved Problem 3.

Name _____

Add. Use counters or drawings to solve.

1 Frankie has 5 cards.
Claudia has 2 cards and Calvin has 3 cards.
How many cards do they have in all?

_10_ cards

2 Michelle has 10 pencils. Jordan has 2 pencils.
Randy has 4 pencils.
How many pencils do they have in all?

_16_ pencils

3 Nina has 9 red buttons.
She has 1 blue button and 2 yellow buttons.
How many buttons does she have in all?

$9 + 1 + 2 = \underline{12}$ _12_ buttons

4 Jackson has 3 red leaves.
He has 1 orange leaf and 7 yellow leaves.
How many leaves does he have in all?

$3 + 1 + 7 = \underline{11}$ _11_ leaves

☆ **Tell about the steps you took to solve Problem 4.**

●●●

Solve.

1 Will has 4 cars.

Ashley has 2 cars and David has 3 cars.

How many cars do they have in all?

_9_ cars

2 Ava has 3 orange leaves.

Dylan has 1 red leaf and 6 yellow leaves.

How many leaves do they have in all?

_10_ leaves

3 First, Dad folds 7 shirts. Then he folds 3 more shirts. Last, he folds 5 shirts.

How many shirts did he fold in all?

$7 + 3 + 5 =$ _15_   _15_ shirts

4 There are 9 pens on the desk. There are 3 pens on the table. There are also 3 pens in the drawer. How many pens are there in all?

$9 + 3 + 3 =$ _15_   _15_ pens

Unit 5
Use Properties of Addition to Add

Standard

Operations and Algebraic Thinking
Represent and solve problems involving addition and subtraction.
1.OA.2 Solve word problems that call for addition of three whole numbers whose sum is less than or equal to 20, e.g., by using objects, drawings, and equations with a symbol for the unknown number to represent the problem.
Understand and apply properties of operations and the relationship between addition and subtraction.
1.OA.3 Apply properties of operations as strategies to add and subtract.

Model the Skill

◆ Hand out 20 connecting cubes (2 different colors, 10 each) for each student and write the following problem on the board.

$$2 + 3 = \underline{\hspace{1cm}}$$

◆ **Say:** *Look at this problem. We will use cubes to solve it.* Have students show each number with a different color cube train. Have them put the trains together. Lay the train across to match the numbers in the equation.

◆ **Ask:** *What is 2 + 3? (5) Let's change the order of the numbers.* Demonstrate how to flip the cube train so the set of 3 is now before the set of 2. Help the students flip the train to show 3 + 2.

$$3 + 2 = \underline{\hspace{1cm}}$$

◆ **Ask:** *What is 3 + 2? (5) 2 + 3 = 5 and 3 + 2 = 5. Why do they both equal the same number? (The numbers you are adding are the same.) 2 + 3 = 5 and 3 + 2 = 5 are related facts. That means they both use the same 3 numbers.* Help students understand that changing the order of the addends does not change the sum.

◆ Assign students the appropriate practice page(s) to support their understanding of the skill. Use cubes to represent the two addends and then flip the cube train to show the related fact.

Assess the Skill

Use the following problems to pre-/post-assess students' understanding of the skill.

$4 + 3 = \underline{\hspace{1cm}}$ $8 + 6 = \underline{\hspace{1cm}}$ $9 + 2 = \underline{\hspace{1cm}}$

$3 + 4 = \underline{\hspace{1cm}}$ $6 + 8 = \underline{\hspace{1cm}}$ $2 + 9 = \underline{\hspace{1cm}}$

Name _____

Use to add.

❶ 2 + 4 = __6__

    4 + 2 = __6__

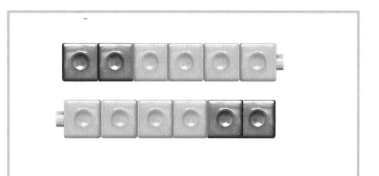

❷ 7 + 3 = __10__

    3 + 7 = __10__

❸ (2 + 3) + 6 = __11__

    ↓

    __5__ + 6 = __11__

    2 + (3 + 6) = __11__

           ↓

    2 + __9__ = __11__

☆ **Circle the number sentences that are equal to 10.**

Name _____

Use . Add the numbers in the ( ) first. Then add.

1 $5 + 3 = \underline{8}$

$3 + 5 = \underline{8}$

$(3 + 2) + 3 = \underline{8}$

$3 + (2 + 3) = \underline{8}$

2

$(6 + 1) + 3 = \underline{\hspace{1cm}}$

$6 + (1 + 3) = \underline{\hspace{1cm}}$

3

$(3 + 9) + 6 = \underline{\hspace{1cm}}$

$3 + (9 + 6) = \underline{\hspace{1cm}}$

4

$(2 + 7) + 4 = \underline{\hspace{1cm}}$

$2 + (7 + 4) = \underline{\hspace{1cm}}$

☆ Tell why **5 + 8** equals **8 + 5.**

Name _____

Use . Add the numbers in the ( ) first. Then add.

1

$(2 + 6) + 4 =$ _____ $2 + (6 + 4) =$ _____

2

$(3 + 4) + 6 =$ _____ $3 + (4 + 6) =$ _____

3

$(6 + 7) + 3 =$ _____ $6 + (7 + 3) =$ _____

4
   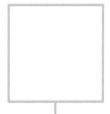

$(7 + 4) + 5 =$ _____ $7 + (4 + 5) =$ _____

☆ **Tell about the steps you took to solve Problem 4.**

Add. Match the number sentences that use the same numbers.

1 Circle the number sentence that is equal to 20.

$$7 + (9 + 4) =$$ $$(1 + 9) + 4 =$$

---

2 Circle the number sentence that is equal to 15.

$$3 + (5 + 7) =$$ $$(8 + 3) + 6 =$$

---

3 Circle the number sentence that is equal to 17.

$$6 + (5 + 7) =$$ $$(8 + 2) + 7 =$$

---

4 Circle the number sentence that is equal to 14.

$$3 + (4 + 6) =$$ $$1 + (9 + 4) =$$

Unit 6
Use Strategies to Add

Standard

> **Operations and Algebraic Thinking**
> **Understand and apply properties of operations and the relationship between addition and subtraction.**
> **1.OA.3** Apply properties of operations as strategies to add and subtract.
> **Add and subtract within 20.**
> **1.OA.5** Relate counting to addition and subtraction.
> **1.OA.6** Add and subtract within 20, demonstrating fluency for addition and subtraction within 10. Use strategies such as counting on; making ten; decomposing a number leading to a ten; using the relationship between addition and subtraction; and creating equivalent but easier or known sums.

Model the Skill

◆ Draw this number line on the board with the following problem.

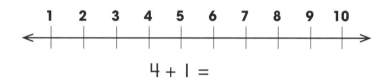

$$4 + 1 =$$

◆ **Say:** *Look at the number line. We will use it to help add by counting on it.* Have students explore the number line and discuss the numbers on it, the order of the numbers, and the end arrows.

◆ **Ask:** *Which is the greater number?* (4) Have students circle it. Then help them find the 4 on the number line. **Say:** *Next we have to add 1.* Demonstrate how to move forward 1 to the next number, 5.

◆ **Ask:** *What number did you land on?* (5) *We started at 4 and added 1 more. We ended at 5. 4 + 1 = 5.* Help students understand that when they move to the right on the number line, the numbers increase by 1 each time. Explain that when they need to add, they need to move to the right.

◆ Assign students the appropriate practice page(s) to support their understanding of the skill. Some students may not need to use the number line.

Assess the Skill

Use the following problems to pre-/post-assess students' understanding of the skill.

$$2 + 4 + 1 = \underline{\quad}$$

$$2 + 3 + 5 = \underline{\quad}$$

$$8 + 6 = 10 + \underline{\quad} = \underline{\quad}$$

Name _____

Circle the greater number in each problem. Count on the number line to add.

1   5 + 2 = _____

2   7 + 1 = _____

3   3 + 3 = _____

4   2 + 8 = _____

☆   Circle the problem where you made 3 "jumps" on the number line.

Circle the greater number. Count on the number line to add.

11   12   13   14   15   16   17   18   19   20

❶ $16 + 1 =$ _____   **❷** $2 + 17 =$ _____

❸ $3 + 13 =$ _____   **❹** $15 + 5 =$ _____

❺ $11 + 3 =$ _____   **❻** $12 + 4 =$ _____

 Tell how you use the number line to add in Problem 5.

Name _____

Use a  and to make 10. Fill in the missing numbers.

ten-frame   counters

❶
$$9 + 3 = 10 + \underline{} = \underline{}$$

❷
$$9 + 7 = 10 + \underline{} = \underline{}$$

❸
$$8 + 6 = 10 + \underline{} = \underline{}$$

❹
$$4 + 7 = 10 + \underline{} = \underline{}$$

❺
$$6 + 5 = 10 + \underline{} = \underline{}$$

❻
$$5 + 8 = 10 + \underline{} = \underline{}$$

☆ **Tell how making 10 helps you add.**

Unit 6 • Common Core Mathematics Grade 1 • ©2012 Newmark Learning, LLC

Name _____

Add. Use counters and a  ten-frame if you like.

❶ Circle the number sentence that is equal to 8 + 7.

$$6 + 10 = 16 \qquad 5 + 10 = 15$$

❷ Circle the number sentence that is equal to 7 + 4.

$$10 + 1 = 11 \qquad 10 + 2 = 12$$

❸ Circle the number sentence that is equal to 9 + 7.

$$10 + 6 = 16 \qquad 10 + 5 = 15$$

❹ Circle the number sentence that is equal to 8 + 6.

$$8 + 2 + 6 = 16 \qquad 8 + 2 + 4 = 14$$

Unit 7
Use Strategies to Subtract

Standard

Operations and Algebraic Thinking

Understand and apply properties of operations and the relationship between addition and subtraction.

1.OA.3 Apply properties of operations as strategies to add and subtract.

1.OA.4 Understand subtraction as an unknown-addend problem.

Add and subtract within 20.

1.OA.5 Relate counting to addition and subtraction

1.OA.6 Add and subtract within 20, demonstrating fluency for addition and subtraction within 10. Use strategies such as counting on; making ten; decomposing a number leading to a ten, using the relationship between addition and subtraction; and creating equivalent but easier or known sums.

Model the Skill

◆ Draw this number line on the board with the following problem.

$$6 - 1 =$$

◆ **Say:** *Look at the number line. We will use it to subtract by counting back. When we subtract, it means we take away. That means that the answers will be less than the starting number.*

◆ **Ask:** *Which direction should we move on the number line to show we are taking away?* (to the left) Explain that the numbers decrease when you move left on a number line.

◆ **Ask:** *What number should you start on?* (6) *How many should you count back?* (1) Have students put their fingers on the 6 and move back 1. Remind them which direction to move. **Ask:** *What number did you end on?* (5) Have them write the number.

◆ Assign students the appropriate practice page(s) to support their understanding of the skill. Watch that students do not count the starting number and that they are moving left on the number line.

Assess the Skill

Use the following problems to pre-/post-assess students' understanding of the skill.

$2 + 4 =$ _____ $7 + 5 =$ _____

$6 - 2 =$ _____ $12 - 7 =$ _____

$6 - 4 =$ _____ $12 - 5 =$ _____

Name _____

Count back to subtract.

1

$$4 - 2 = \underline{\hspace{2cm}}$$

2

$$7 - 5 = \underline{\hspace{2cm}}$$

3

$$9 - 3 = \underline{\hspace{2cm}}$$

4

$$10 - 3 = \underline{\hspace{2cm}}$$

 Draw a number line.

Name _____

Count back to subtract.

1 20 – 1 = __19__

2 14 – 2 = __12__

3 16 – 3 = __13__

4 19 – 3 = __16__

5 18 – 4 = __14__

6 17 – 6 = __11__

☆ **Tell how you use the number line to subtract.**

Name _____

Use . Write the number sentences.

1 6   1

6 + 1 = 7   6 - 1 = 5

2 3   5

3 + 5 = 8   3 - 5 2

3 7   3

7 + 3 = 10   7 - 3 = 4

4 6   5

6 + 5 = 11   6 - 5 = 1

5 7   4

7 + 4 = 11   7 - 4 = 3

6 8   9

8 + 9 = 18   8 - 9 = 1

☆   **How do addition facts help you subtract?**

Solve.

1 Clare has 12 books.
She gives 5 books to Ava.
How many books does Clare have left?

$$12 - 5 = \underline{}$$

2 Jacob has 10 cars.
He gives 2 away.
How many does he have left?

$$10 - 2 = \underline{}$$

3 Kaya has 18 stamps.
She uses 9 stamps.
How many stamps does she have left?

$$18 - 9 = \underline{}$$

4 Josh has 11 balloons.
4 balloons pop.
How many balloons does he have left?

$$11 - 4 = \underline{}$$

Unit 8
Find the Missing Number

Standard

Operations and Algebraic Thinking
Work with addition and subtraction equations.
1.OA.7 Understand the meaning of the equal sign, and determine if equations involving addition and subtraction are true or false.
1.OA.8 Determine the unknown whole number in an addition or subtraction equation relating three whole numbers.

Model the Skill

◆ Write the following equations on the board.

$$2 = 1 + 1 \qquad 7 - 1 = 6$$

$$3 = 4 + 1 \qquad 8 - 3 = 4$$

$$3 + 1 = 4 \qquad 8 - 3 = 5$$

◆ Explain that an equation shows two expressions, one on each side of an equal sign, that are equal. **Say:** *Look at the equations. We will find which are true and which are false.* Point to 2 = 1 + 1. Instruct students to find the equal sign and then look at both sides of it.

◆ **Ask:** *Do both sides show the same amount?* (yes) *If both sides have the same amount, it is true.* Ask what other equations on the board are true.

◆ Have students look at 3 = 4 + 1. **Ask:** *Do both sides show the same amount?* (no) *If both sides do not have the same amount, it is false.* Ask what other equations on the board are false.

◆ Assign students the appropriate practice page(s) to support their understanding of the skill. Point out that the equal sign can be in different places in an equation.

Assess the Skill

Use the following problems to pre-/post-assess students' understanding of the skill.

◆ **Say:** *Look at each equation. Tell whether each one is true or false. Do both sides show the same amount?*

$$12 = 12 \qquad\qquad 7 + 6 = 6 + 7$$

$$5 + 6 = 12 \qquad\qquad 9 - 4 = 3 + 3$$

Name _____

Fill in the missing number.

1

$$7 + \underline{\quad} = 10$$

2

$$11 - 2 = \underline{\quad}$$

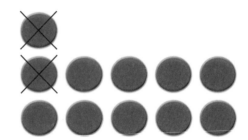

3

$$7 = 3 + \underline{\quad}$$

4

$$5 = \underline{\quad} - 3$$

☆ **Circle the counters that also show 5 + 3 = 8.**

●○○

Name _____

Fill in the missing number.

1 7 + 4 = _____

2 11 = _____ − 4

3 12 − 2 = _____

4 8 + 2 = ☐

5 7 = 3 + _____

6 20 − ☐ = 19

 Tell how you solved Problem 5.

Name _____

Fill in the missing number.

❶ $3 + 4 =$ _____

❷ $6 - 4 =$ _____

❸ $12 -$ _____ $= 9$

❹ $11 -$ _____ $= 7$

❺ _____ $+ 7 = 15$

❻ _____ $+ 5 = 13$

❼ $13 = 6 +$ _____

❽ $3 = 6 -$ _____

☆ **Tell how you could use subtraction to solve Problem 6.**

●●●

Fill in the missing number.

1 Jill has 6 blocks.
Tyler has some blocks.
They have 15 blocks in all.
How many blocks does Tyler have?

$$6 + \underline{\hspace{1.5cm}} = 15$$

2 Linda has 12 jars. She breaks some.
She has 9 left. How many jars broke?

$$12 - \underline{\hspace{1.5cm}} = 9$$

3 You and I have 14 trucks.
You have 8 trucks.
How many trucks do I have?

$$8 + \underline{\hspace{1.5cm}} = 14$$

4 There are 16 cupcakes.
We eat some. Then there are 9 left.
How many did we eat?

$$16 - \underline{\hspace{1.5cm}} = 9$$

Unit 9
Count, Read, and Write Numbers to 120

Standard

Number and Operations in Base Ten
Extend the counting sequence.
1.NBT.1 Count to 120, starting at any number less than 120. In this range, read and write numerals and represent a number of objects with a written numeral.

Model the Skill

◆ Display a hundred chart or provide charts for each student.

◆ **Say:** *Look at this chart. It is a hundred chart. It shows the numbers in order to 100.* Have the class read the numbers across the top row. **Ask:** *Where do we go to find the next number?* (down to the next row) Show students where to find the next number and continue counting to 50.

◆ Write the following counting sequence (with blanks) on the board.

$$22, \underline{\quad}, \underline{\quad}, 25, 26, 27, \underline{\quad}, \underline{\quad}, 30$$

◆ **Say:** *Look at this row of numbers. Some numbers are missing.* Read the numbers and use the word "blank" when appropriate. **Say:** *We will read the numbers and say the next counting number when we see a blank.*

◆ **Ask:** *What number did we say after 22?* (23) *Let's fill it in. What number did we say after 27?* (28) *Let's fill it in.* Help students write the missing numbers.

◆ Assign students the appropriate practice page(s) to support their understanding of the skill.

Assess the Skill

Use the following problem to pre-/post-assess students' understanding of the skill.

◆ **Say:** *Look at each set. Tell which one is in order.*

| 45 | 46 | 47 | 48 | 49 | | 108 | 109 | 110 | 111 | 112 | 113 |

| 48 | 45 | 47 | 49 | 46 | | 108 | 109 | 110 | 111 | 113 | 114 |

Name _____

For each problem, count forward. Write the missing numbers.

1

12	13	14	15	16	17

2

24	25	26	27	28	29

3

80	81	82	83	84	85

4

98	99	100	101	102	103

☆ **Circle the number between 83 and 85.**

Name _____

For each problem, count forward. Write the missing numbers.

1

| 70 | 71 | 72 | 73 | 74 | 75 |

2

| 61 | 62 | 63 | 64 | 65 | 66 |

3

| 87 | 88 | 89 | 90 | 91 | 92 |

4

| 95 | 96 | 97 | 98 | 99 | 100 |

5

| 105 | 106 | 107 | 108 | 109 | 110 |

6

| 113 | 114 | 115 | 116 | 117 | 118 |

☆ **Tell how you know what number comes next.**

For each problem, read the numbers in each set. Circle the sets that are in order.

1

| 55 | 56 | 57 | 58 | 59 |

| 58 | 55 | 57 | 59 | 56 |

2

| 64 | 65 | 66 | 67 | 86 |

| 64 | 65 | 66 | 67 | 68 |

3

| 99 | 101 | 100 | 103 | 102 |

| 98 | 99 | 100 | 101 | 102 |

4

| 116 | 117 | 118 | 120 | 119 |

| 116 | 117 | 118 | 119 | 120 |

5

| 108 | 109 | 110 | 111 | 112 |

| 108 | 109 | 110 | 111 | 113 |

6

| 106 | 107 | 108 | 109 | 101 |

| 106 | 107 | 108 | 109 | 110 |

 Tell how you know which sets are in order.

Name _____

1 Count aloud from 83 to 88. Then fill in the missing numbers.

| 83 | 84 | 85 | 86 | 87 | 88 |

2 Count aloud from 46 to 51. Then fill in the missing numbers.

| 46 | 47 | 48 | 49 | 50 | 51 |

3 Count aloud from 115 to 120. Then fill in the missing numbers.

| 115 | 116 | 117 | 118 | 119 | 120 |

4 Circle the number that is missing from 75, 76, 77, 79, 80, 81, 82.

79   77   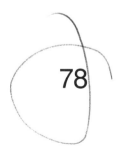78

Unit 10
Tens and Ones

Standard

Number and Operations in Base Ten
Understand place value.
1.NBT.2 Understand that the two digits of a two-digit number represent amounts of tens and ones. Understand: 10 can be thought of as a bundle of ten ones — called a "ten"; the numbers from 11 to 19 are composed of a ten and one, two, three, four, five, six, seven, eight, or nine ones; the numbers 10, 20, 30, 40, 50, 60, 70, 80, 90 refer to one, two, three, four, five, six, seven, eight, or nine tens (and 0 ones).

Model the Skill

◆ Hand out ten-frames and 15 counters to each student.

◆ **Say:** *Look at the ten-frame. Let's count how many counters are in it. 1, 2, 3, 4, 5, 6, 7, 8, 9, 10. Let's fill a ten-frame.* Help students count out 10 counters and fill their ten-frames. **Say:** *We have 10 ones or we can say we have 1 ten.* Point out the "1 ten" under the ten-frame.

◆ **Say:** *Now I will add one more counter. Does it fit? How many extra counters do I have?* (1) Help students model it by putting one more counter next to their frames. **Say:** *We have 1 more or we can say we have 1 one.* Point out the "1 one." *We have 1 ten and 1 one. How many are there in all?* (11) Help students count and write the number.

◆ Assign students the appropriate practice page(s) to support their understanding of the skill. Encourage modeling the problems, then counting how many tens and ones, and writing how many in all.

◆ Help students realize that the two digits of the two-digit number represent the amounts of tens and ones.

Assess the Skill

Use the following problems to pre-/post-assess students' understanding of the skill.

◆ Hand out base-ten blocks. **Say:** *Look at each number.* Use base ten blocks to form each number. Tell how many tens and ones are in each number.

14   73   26   81   60   5

Name _____

For each problem, use a ⬚⬚⬚⬚⬚ and ⚪⚪ . Count and write how many.
ten-frame   counters

1

I ten   I one _____

2

I ten   2 ones _____

3

I ten   3 ones _____

4

I ten   4 ones _____

 Tell how many ones are on this page.

●○○   Unit 10 • Common Core Mathematics Grade 1 • ©2012 Newmark Learning, LLC

Name _____

For each problem, count how many. Record your work.

1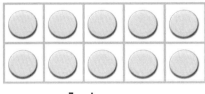

1 ten _____ ones _____

2

1 ten _____ ones _____

3

1 ten _____ ones _____

4

1 ten _____ ones _____

5

1 ten _____ ones _____

 Tell how many tens are on this page.

Name _____

For each problem, count how many. Record your work.

1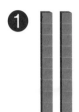

_2_ tens _0_ ones

_20_

2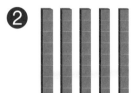

_5_ tens _0_ ones

_50_

3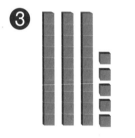

_3_ tens _5_ ones

_35_

4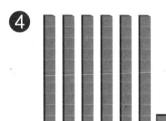

_6_ tens _1_ one's

_61_

5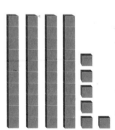

_4_ tens _6_ ones

_46_

6

_7_ tens _4_ ones

_74_

☆ **Tell how you solved Problem 6.**

●●●

Name _____

Solve.

1 How many tens?

_____

2 How many ones?

_____

3 How many tens?

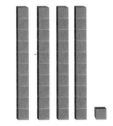

_____

4 How many ones?

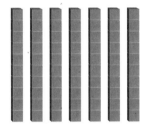

_____

5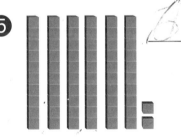

_6___ tens

_____ ones

_____

6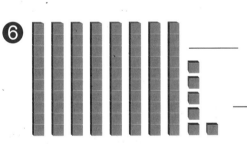

_____ tens

_____ ones

_____

7 How many tens are in the number 67?

8 How many ones are in the number 80?

Unit 11
Compare Numbers

Standard

Number and Operations in Base Ten
Understand place value.

1.NBT.2 Understand that the two digits of a two-digit number represent amounts of tens and ones.

1.NBT.3 Compare two two-digit numbers based on meanings of the tens and ones digits, recording the results of comparisons with the symbols >, =, and <.

Model the Skill

◆ **Say:** *Today we will compare numbers. There are special signs used to compare numbers.* Draw a "greater than" sign: >, a "less than" sign: <, and an "equal to" sign: =. Name each sign as you draw it.

◆ Explain to students that to compare numbers, first they have to look at the number of tens. The number that has more tens is greater, making the other number less. **Ask:** *Is 23 greater than, less than, or equal to 58?* (less than, <) Help the students write the less than sign. Explain that the pointy side always points to the lesser number and the large mouth side opens to the greater number.

◆ Assign students the appropriate practice page(s) to support their understanding of the skill. Explain that when the tens are the same, they need to compare the ones, and if the ones are also the same, the numbers are equal.

Assess the Skill

Use the following problems to pre-/post-assess students' understanding of the skill.

◆ **Say:** *Look at each expression. Tell if each one is true or false.*

$$14 < 16 \qquad 36 = 26 \qquad 81 > 18 \qquad 56 > 72$$

Name _____

For each problem, compare. Write >, =, or <.

is greater than	>
is equal to	=
is less than	<

1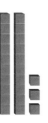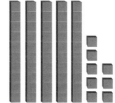

23   58

2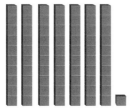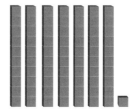

71   71

3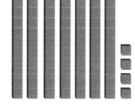

49   74

4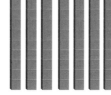

86   82

 Circle the greatest number on this page.

Name _____

is greater than	>
is equal to	=
is less than	<

For each problem, underline the tens digits.
Compare. Write >, =, or <.

1

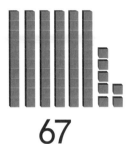
67

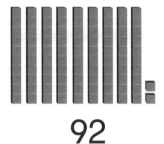
92

2

26   26

3

58   54

4

31   13

 Tell how you know when two numbers are equal.

●●○

Name _____

For each problem, underline the tens digits.
Circle the ones digit. Compare.

is greater than	>
is equal to	=
is less than	<

1 42 48

2 39 14

3 69 69

4 40 73

5 74 78

6 56 56

 Tell how you know which number is greater.

Name _____

For each problem, compare. Write >, =, or <.

1 Write a number that is greater than 67?

68

2 Write a number that is less than 34?

33

3 Write a number that is greater than 59?

60

4 Write a number that is equal to 98?

98

Unit 12
Add a Two-Digit Number and a One-Digit Number

Standard

> **Number and Operations in Base Ten**
> **Use place value understanding and properties of operations to add and subtract.**
> **1.NBT.4** Add within 100, including adding a two-digit number and a one-digit number, and adding a two-digit number and a multiple of 10, using concrete models or drawings and strategies based on place value, properties of operations, and/or the relationship between addition and subtraction; relate the strategy to a written method and explain the reasoning used. Understand that in adding two-digit numbers, one adds tens and tens, ones and ones; and sometimes it is necessary to compose a ten.
> **1.NBT.5** Given a two-digit number, mentally find 10 more or 10 less than the number, without having to count; explain the reasoning used.
> **1.NBT.6** Subtract multiples of 10 in the range 10-90 from multiples of 10 in the range 10-90 (positive or zero differences), using concrete models or drawings and strategies based on place value, properties of operations, and/or the relationship between addition and subtraction; relate the strategy to a written method and explain the reasoning used.

Model the Skill

◆ Hand out base-ten blocks. Then demonstrate the following problem.

$$13 + 2 =$$

$$\begin{array}{r} 13 \\ + \ 2 \end{array}$$

◆ **Say:** *Today we are going to add to find the sum or total. Look at the models of tens and ones. The rod shows 10. The single units show ones. How many ones are there in all?* (5) Remind students of different strategies they can use to add the ones: count units, count on, or add. Help students record the ones in the vertical addition in the correct place.

◆ **Ask:** *How many tens are there in all?* (1) Record the tens. **Say:** *What is the sum of 13 + 2?* (15) Help students understand how the models and vertical addition connect. They may solve in other ways.

◆ Assign students the appropriate practice page(s) to support their understanding of the skill. Allow students to use manipulatives as needed.

Assess the Skill

Use the following problems to pre-/post-assess students' understanding of the skill.

$$\begin{array}{r} 14 \\ + \ 5 \end{array} \qquad \begin{array}{r} 23 \\ + \ 4 \end{array} \qquad \begin{array}{r} 64 \\ + \ 2 \end{array} \qquad \begin{array}{r} 78 \\ + \ 6 \end{array}$$

Name _____

Use base-ten blocks. Find the sum for each problem.

1 $15 + 2 = 17$

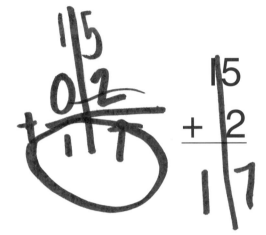

$\begin{array}{r} 15 \\ + 2 \\ \hline 17 \end{array}$

2 $35 + 38 = 38$

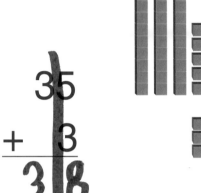

$\begin{array}{r} 35 \\ + 3 \\ \hline 38 \end{array}$

3 $61 + 7$

$\begin{array}{r} 61 \\ + 7 \\ \hline \end{array}$

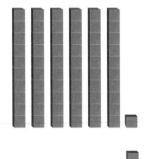

☆ **Write or draw another way to show Problem 1.**

● ○ ○

Name _____

Use base-ten blocks. Add to find the sum.

❶ 39 + 3

$$39$$
$$+\ \ 3$$

❷ 46 + 5

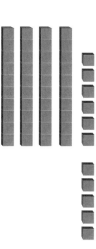

$$46$$
$$+\ \ 5$$

---

❸ 58 + 4

$$58$$
$$+\ \ 4$$

❹ 65 + 6

$$65$$
$$+\ \ 6$$

 Tell how you regrouped the ones in Problem 2.

Name _____

Find the sum for each problem.

1 14 + 5

tens	ones
1	4
+	5

2 30 + 6

tens	ones
+	

3 65 + 4

tens	ones
+	

4 51 + 7

tens	ones
+	

5 85 + 5

tens	ones
+	

6 19 + 6

tens	ones
+	

☆ **Tell how you know which column to put each digit in.**

●●●

Name _____

Find the sum for each problem.

1 Find the sum of 29 and 5.

tens	ones

+

2 Find the sum of 38 and 6.

tens	ones

+

3 Find the sum of 43 and 3.

tens	ones

+

4 Find the sum of 67 and 2.

tens	ones

+

5 Find the sum of 82 and 8.

tens	ones

+

6 Find the sum of 91 and 1.

tens	ones

+

Unit 13
Ten More, Ten Less

Standard

Number and Operations in Base Ten
Use place value understanding and properties of operations to add and subtract.

1.NBT.4 Add within 100, including adding a two-digit number and a one-digit number, and adding a two-digit number and a multiple of 10, using concrete models or drawings and strategies based on place value, properties of operations, and/or the relationship between addition and subtraction; relate the strategy to a written method and explain the reasoning used. Understand that in adding two-digit numbers, one adds tens and tens, ones and ones; and sometimes it is necessary to compose a ten.

1.NBT.5 Given a two-digit number, mentally find 10 more or 10 less than the number, without having to count; explain the reasoning used.

Model the Skill

◆ Hand out ten-rods and ones. Then demonstrate the following problem.

$$24 + 10 =$$

$$\begin{array}{r} 24 \\ + 10 \\ \hline \end{array}$$

◆ **Say:** *Today we are going to add ten to numbers. Look at this problem.* **Ask:** *How many tens are there in 20?* (2) *How many tens are there in 10?* (1)

◆ Explain to students that they are adding 1 to the tens digits when they add 10 to a number. Tell them if they know 2 + 1 = 3, then they should know 20 + 10.

◆ **Ask:** *If we have 2 tens and 1 ten, how many tens are there in all?* (3)

◆ Point out that the first number has 4 ones. Explain that since they are adding 10, they should think of it as 1 ten and 0 ones so only the tens digit will change and the ones digit will stay the same. **Ask:** *What is 24 + 10?* (34)

◆ Assign students the appropriate practice page(s) to support their understanding of the skill. Remind them they are adding or subtracting 1 ten each time.

Assess the Skill

Use the following problems to pre-/post-assess students' understanding of the skill.

$$\begin{array}{r} 20 \\ + 10 \\ \hline \end{array} \qquad \begin{array}{r} 34 \\ + 10 \\ \hline \end{array} \qquad \begin{array}{r} 73 \\ + 10 \\ \hline \end{array} \qquad \begin{array}{r} 11 \\ + 10 \\ \hline \end{array}$$

Name _____

For each problem, find the sum or difference.

1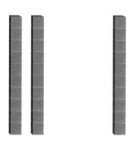

20 + 10 = _30_____

2

13 + 10 = __2 3_____

3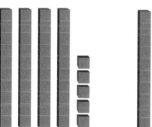

45 + 10 = __55_____

4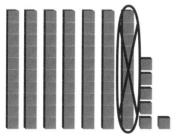

76 − 10 = __66_____

 Circle the answer that shows 2 tens.

Name _____

Find the sum or difference for each problem.

1

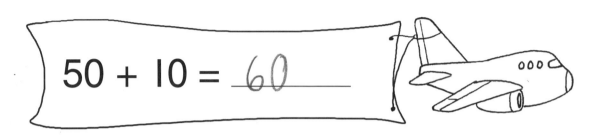

50 + 10 = _60_

2

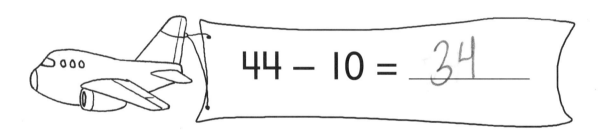

36 + 10 = _46_

3

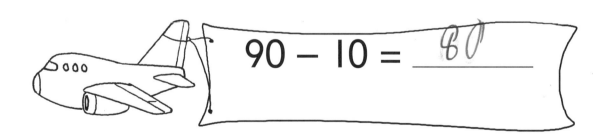

44 – 10 = _34_

4

90 – 10 = _80_

☆ **Tell how you solved Problem 3.**

Name _____

Find the sum or difference for each problem.

❶ $30 + 10 = 4$

❷ $70 - 10 = 60$

❸ $61 - 10 = 51$

❹ $83 + 10 = 93$

❺ $75 + 10 = 85$

❻ $16 - 10 = 6$

  Tell how you add or take away ten.

Name _____

Find the sum or difference for each problem.

1 What is the sum of 10 and 67?

2 What is ten less than 44?

3 Randi had 38 stickers. She got ten more.
How many stickers does Randi have now?

4 Robin had 18 grapes. She ate 10 grapes.
How many grapes does Robin have left?

Unit 14
Add Multiples of Ten

Number and Operations in Base Ten
Use place value understanding and properties of operations to add and subtract.
1.NBT.4 Add within 100, including adding a two-digit number and a one-digit number, and adding a two-digit number and a multiple of 10, using concrete models or drawings and strategies based on place value, properties of operations, and/or the relationship between addition and subtraction; relate the strategy to a written method and explain the reasoning used. Understand that in adding two-digit numbers, one adds tens and tens, ones and ones; and sometimes it is necessary to compose a ten.

Model the Skill

◆ Hand out base-ten blocks and write the following problems on the board.

$$10 + 10 =$$
$$42 + 30 =$$

◆ **Say:** *Today we are going to add to find the sum.* Remind students that the rods show 10. Review different strategies they can use to add: add, count, count on, or use a fact they know.

◆ **Say:** *Write these problems on a piece of paper. Then use your blocks to show 10 + 10.* Have them put the rods together to add. **Ask:** *How many ones are there in all?* (0) *Record the ones. How many tens are there in all?* (2) *Record the tens. What is the sum of 10 + 10?* (20)

◆ Have students look at the next problem and model it. Remind them that when adding a number with two or more digits, they should always add the ones first. **Say:** *How many ones are there in all?* (2) *How many tens are there in all?* (7) *What is the sum of 42 + 30?* (72)

◆ Assign students the appropriate practice page(s) to support their understanding of the skill.

Assess the Skill

Use the following problems to pre-/post-assess students' understanding of the skill.

20	54	33	21
+ 30	+ 20	+ 40	+ 70

Name _____

For each problem, use base-ten models. Find the sum.

1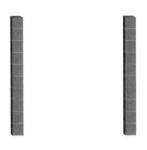

10   +   10

$$\begin{array}{r} 10 \\ +\ 10 \\ \hline 20 \end{array}$$

2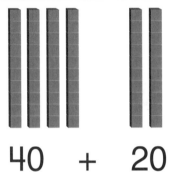

40   +   20

$$\begin{array}{r} 40 \\ +\ 20 \\ \hline 60 \end{array}$$

3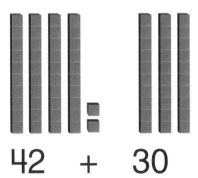

42   +   30

$$\begin{array}{r} 42 \\ +\ 30 \\ \hline 72 \end{array}$$

4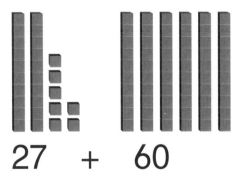

27   +   60

$$\begin{array}{r} 27 \\ +\ 60 \\ \hline 87 \end{array}$$

☆   **Circle the problem that shows 6 tens in all.**

●○○

Name _____

Find the sum for each problem.

1

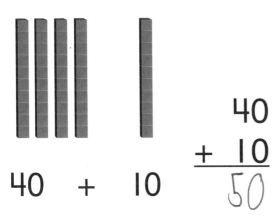

40 + 10

$$\begin{array}{r} 40 \\ +\ 10 \\ \hline 50 \end{array}$$

2 35 + 40

tens	ones
3	5
+ 4	0

75

3 19 + 70

tens	ones
1	9
+ 7	0

8   9

4 54 + 40 = 94

  Tell how you solved Problem 4.

Name _____

Find the sum for each problem.

❶ 30 + 20

tens	ones
3	0
+ 2	0
5	0

❷ 60 + 30

tens	ones
6	0
+ 3	0
9	0

❸ 20 + 20

tens	ones
2	0
+ 2	0
4	0

❹ 51 + 20

tens	ones
5	1
+ 2	0
7	1

❺ 65 + 30

tens	ones
6	5
+ 3	0
9	5

❻ 19 + 40

tens	ones
1	9
+ 4	0
5	9

☆ **Tell how you add multiples of ten.**

Name _____

Find the sum for each problem.

❶ Find the sum of 73 and 10.

tens	ones
7	3
1	0
8	3

❷ Find the sum of 66 and 20.

tens	ones
6	6
2	0
8	6

❸ Find the sum of 50 and 30.

tens	ones
5	0
3	0
8	0

❹ Find the sum of 23 and 40.

tens	ones
2	3
4	0
6	3

❺ What is the sum of 25 and 50?

tens	ones
2	5
5	0
7	5

❻ What is the sum of 17 and 60?

tens	ones
1	7
6	0
7	7

Unit 15
Subtract Multiples of Ten

Number and Operations in Base Ten
Use place value understanding and properties of operations to add and subtract.
1.NBT.6. Subtract multiples of 10 in the range 10-90 from multiples of 10 in the range 10-90 (positive or zero differences), using concrete models or drawings and strategies based on place value, properties of operations, and/or the relationship between addition and subtraction; relate the strategy to a written method and explain the reasoning used.

Model the Skill

◆ Hand out base-ten blocks and draw the following problem on the board.

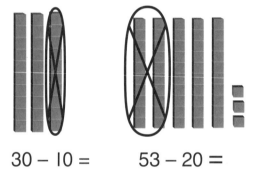

$$30 - 10 = \qquad 53 - 20 =$$

◆ **Say:** *Today we are going to subtract. Look at the models for this problem.* Explain that the first number, 30, is how many in all. Use your blocks to show 30.

◆ Tell students that the number being taken away is circled and crossed out with an X. **Ask:** *How many do you have to take away?* (10) Have students take away 1 ten. **Ask:** *How many ones are there?* (0) *How many tens are left?* (2) *What is 30 – 10?* (20)

◆ Have students look at the next problem and model it. Remind them that when subtracting a number with two or more digits, they should always subtract the ones first. **Ask:** *What is 3 – 0?* (3) Have students record the ones. **Ask:** *What is 5 – 2?* (3) Have students record the tens. **Ask:** *What is 53 – 20?* (33)

◆ Assign students the appropriate practice page(s) to support their understanding of the skill.

Assess the Skill

Use the following problems to pre-/post-assess students' understanding of the skill.

$$\begin{array}{r} 30 \\ -20 \\ \hline \end{array} \qquad \begin{array}{r} 54 \\ -40 \\ \hline \end{array} \qquad \begin{array}{r} 73 \\ -50 \\ \hline \end{array} \qquad \begin{array}{r} 91 \\ -70 \\ \hline \end{array}$$

Name _____

For each problem, use base-ten models. Subtract.

1

20   –   10

$$\begin{array}{r} 20 \\ -\ 10 \\ \hline 10 \end{array}$$

2

40   –   20

$$\begin{array}{r} 40 \\ -\ 20 \\ \hline 20 \end{array}$$

3

61   –   30

$$\begin{array}{r} 61 \\ -\ 30 \\ \hline 31 \end{array}$$

4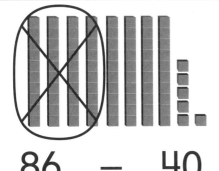

86   –   40

$$\begin{array}{r} 86 \\ -\ 40 \\ \hline 46 \end{array}$$

  Circle the answer that shows 3 tens.

Name _____

Subtract to solve each problem.

1 40 – 10

tens	ones
4	0
− 1	0

3   0

2 70 – 20

tens	ones
7	0
− 2	0

5   0

3 91 – 30

tens	ones
9	1
− 3	0

6   1

4 64 – 50

tens	ones
6	4
− 5	0

1   4

 Tell how you solved Problem 4.

●●○

Name _____

Subtract to solve each problem.

❶ 30 − 20

tens	ones
3	0
− 2	0
1	0

❷ 50 − 30

tens	ones
5	0
− 3	0
2	0

❸ 84 − 30

tens	ones
8	4
− 3	0
5	4

❹ 92 − 50

tens	ones
9	2
− 5	0
4	2

❺ 67 − 20

tens	ones
6	7
− 2	0
4	7

❻ 86 − 80

tens	ones
8	6
− 8	0
0	6

☆ **Tell how you know which column to put each digit in.**

79

Name _____

Subtract for each problem.

1 What is 42 minus 10?

tens	ones
4	2
− 1	0
3	2

2 What is 37 minus 20?

tens	ones
3	7
− 2	0
1	7

3 What is 98 minus 30?

tens	ones
9	8
− 3	0
6	8

4 What is 73 minus 50?

tens	ones
7	3
− 5	0
2	3

5 Find the difference
between 27 and 20.

tens	ones
2	7
− 2	0
0	7

6 Find the difference
between 49 and 30.

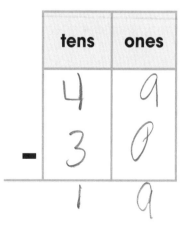

tens	ones
4	9
− 3	0
1	9

☆ **Tell how you solved the last problem.**

Unit 16
Compare and Order Lengths

Standard

> **Measurement and Data**
> **Measure lengths indirectly and by iterating length units.**
> **1.MD.1** Order three objects by length; compare the lengths of two objects indirectly by using a third object.
> **1.MD.2** Express the length of an object as a whole number of length units, by laying multiple copies of a shorter object (the length unit) end to end; understand that the length measurement of an object is the number of same-size length units that span it with no gaps or overlaps. Limit to contexts where the object being measured is spanned by a whole number of length units with no gaps or overlaps.

Model the Skill

◆ Draw two lines of different lengths on the board.

◆ **Say:** *Today we will compare objects to see which is longer and which is shorter. Look at the two lines.* Point out that both of their ends start against the same starting line. Explain that to compare lengths, students need to put the ends of objects at the same place.

◆ **Say:** *To find which line is longer, you need to find which sticks out farther. Which line is longer?* Circle it. **Say:** *To find which is shorter, you need to find which does not stick out as far or which ends closer to the line where they started. Which line is shorter?* Draw an X next to it.

◆ Assign students the appropriate practice page(s) to support their understanding of the skill.

Assess the Skill

Use the following activity to pre-/post-assess students' understanding of the skill.

◆ **Say:** *Look at the door. Is the door longer from side to side or top to bottom?* Repeat with other items in the classroom. Then ask groups of students to line themselves up in order of height.

Name _____

For each problem, circle the longer object. Underline the shorter object.

 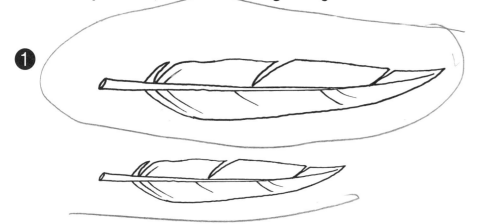

 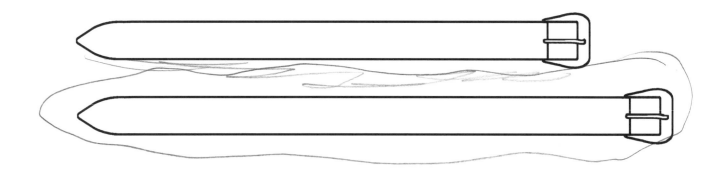

 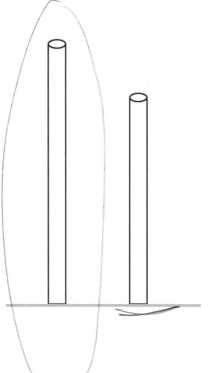

☆ **Put an X on the longest item on the page.**

●○○

Name _____

For each problem, order the pictures from shortest to longest.

1

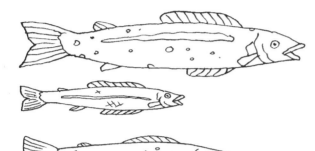

3

1

2

2

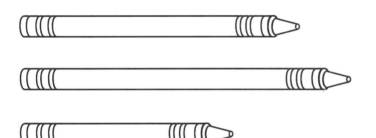

2

3

1

3

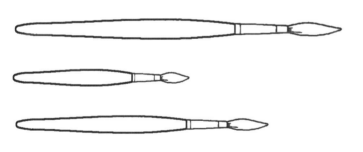

3

1

2

4

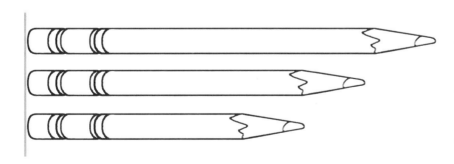

3

2

1

☆ **Tell how you know which item is the shortest.**

Name _____

For each problem, order the pictures from longest to shortest.

1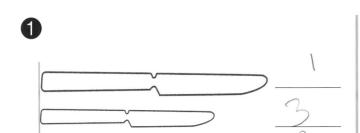

1
3
2

2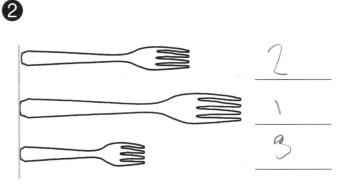

2
1
3

3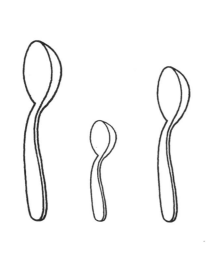

1 3 2

4

2 3 1

☆ Tell how you know which item is the longest.

Name _____

Use string. Measure the length of each real object in your classroom.

board

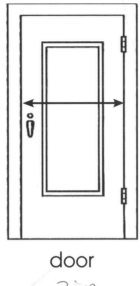

door

table

4 in

3 in

4 in

1 Which is the shortest?

3 door

2 Which is the longest?

board   table

3 Put them in order from shortest to longest.

door, board, table

☆ **Tell how you compared each string to find the answers.**

Unit 17
Measure Length with Non-Standard Units

Standard

Measurement and Data
Measure lengths indirectly and by iterating length units.

1.MD.2 Express the length of an object as a whole number of length units, by laying multiple copies of a shorter object (the length unit) end to end; understand that the length measurement of an object is the number of same-size length units that span it with no gaps or overlaps.

Model the Skill

◆ Hand out unsharpened pencils and paper clips of equal size and length.

◆ **Say:** *Today we will measure the length of objects. We will use paper clips to measure.* Point out that all the clips are exactly the same size because when you use objects to measure, the objects all must be exactly the same size.

◆ **Say:** *To measure how long the pencil is, we will place the clips below it from the beginning to the end.* Model how to place the first clip at the very beginning of the pencil, and have students do the same.

◆ **Ask:** *Are we at the end of the pencil yet?* (no) Demonstrate how to place the next clip touching but not overlapping the first clip. **Ask:** *Have we reached the end yet?* (no) Add clips until they have reached the end of the pencil. **Ask:** *How many clips long is the pencil?* (about 6 small paper clips or 4 large paper clips)

◆ Assign students the appropriate practice page(s) to support their understanding of the skill.

Assess the Skill

Use the following activity to pre-/post-assess students' understanding of the skill.

◆ Hand out paper clips.
◆ **Say:** *Use the paper clips to measure objects.*
What is the length of your desk in paper clips?
What is the length of your shoe in paper clips?.

Name _____

Cut out the boxes. For each problem, use the boxes to measure. Record your work.

1

The crayon is about _____ 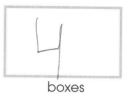 long.

boxes

2

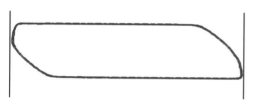

Tthe eraser is about _____  long.

boxes

3

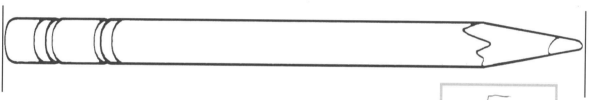

The pencil is about _____  long.

boxes

4

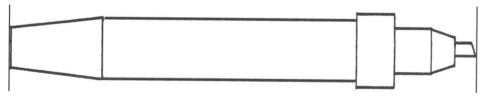

The marker is about _____  long.

boxes

☆ **Circle the item that was the shortest.**

Name _____

Cut out the boxes. For each problem, use the boxes to measure.
Record your work.

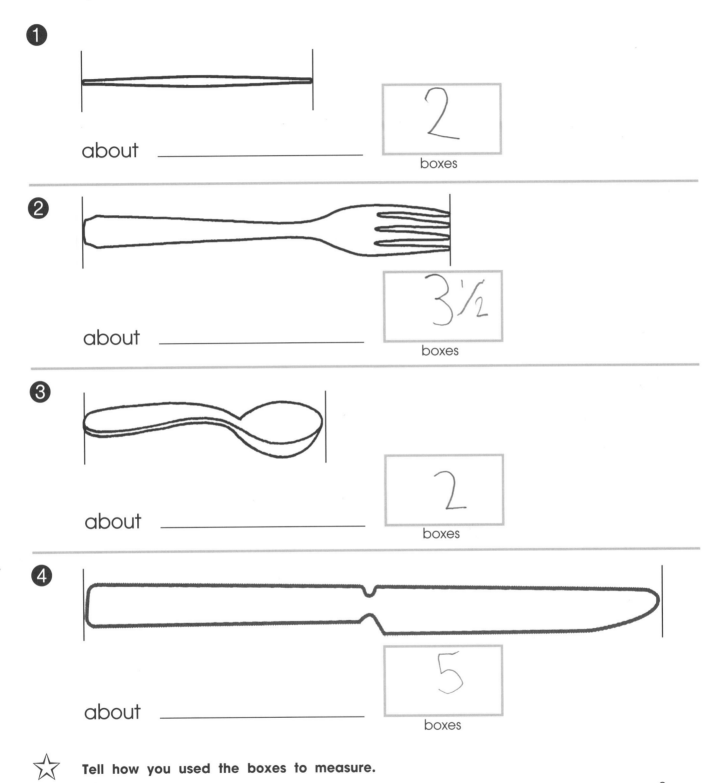

1

about _____ 2 boxes

2

about _____ 3½ boxes

3

about _____ 2 boxes

4

about _____ 5 boxes

☆ Tell how you used the boxes to measure.

●●● rk Learning, LLC

Name _____

For each problem, use small to measure. Record your work.

paper clips

1

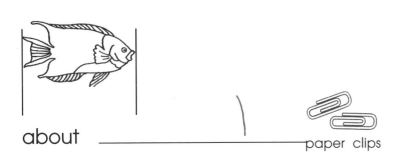

about _____ \ paper clips

2

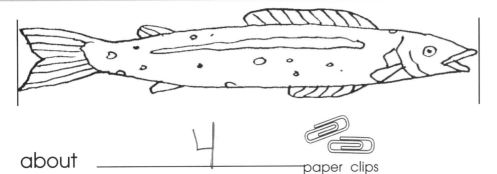

about _____ 4 paper clips

3

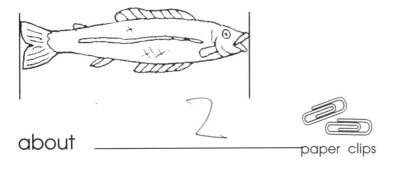

about _____ 2 paper clips

4

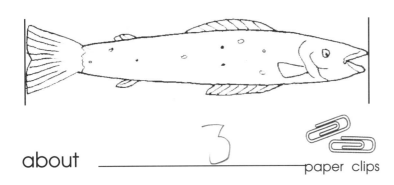

about _____ 3 paper clips

☆ **Tell how you used paper clips to measure.**

For each problem, use small to measure. Record your work.

paper clips

1 About how long is this hair pin?

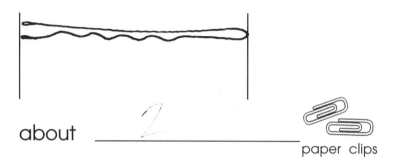

about _____ *2* _____ paper clips

---

2 About how long is this comb?

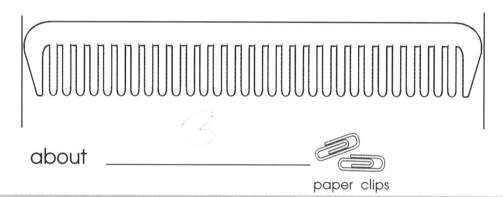

about _____ paper clips

---

3 About how long is this brush?

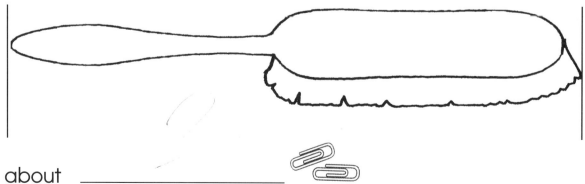

about _____ paper clips

Unit 18
Tell and Write Time

Measurement and Data
Tell and write time.
1.MD.3 Tell and write time in hours and half-hours using analog and
digital clocks.

Model the Skill

◆ Draw the following clock on the board.

◆ **Say:** *Look at the clock. A clock has an hour hand and a minute hand. It also has 12 numbers.* Help students point to each number as you say them aloud from 1 to 12. Explain that the hands move in the same direction as the numbers.

◆ **Say:** *The short hand tells the hour. The long hand tells the minutes. When the long or minute hand is straight up on the 12, we say the time as o'clock.*

◆ **Ask:** *What number is the hour hand on?* (2) *What number is the minute hand on?* (12) Explain that it means it is exactly on the hour and we will say o'clock. **Ask:** *What time is it?* (2 o'clock)

◆ Assign students the appropriate practice page(s) to support their understanding

Use the following clock faces to pre-/post-assess students' understanding of the skill.

Assess the Skill

◆ **Say:** *Look at each clock. What time does each clock show?*

Name _____

For each problem, draw a line to the clock that shows the same time.

❶

❷

❸

❹

 Circle a time when you are not at school.

●○○

Name _____

For each problem, look at each clock. Tell and write the time.

1

2:00

2

5:00

3
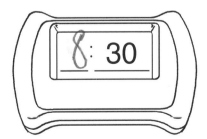
8: 30

4
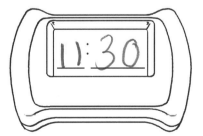
11:30

 Tell how you know when it is 2 o'clock.

Name _____

For each problem, look at each clock. Tell and write the time.

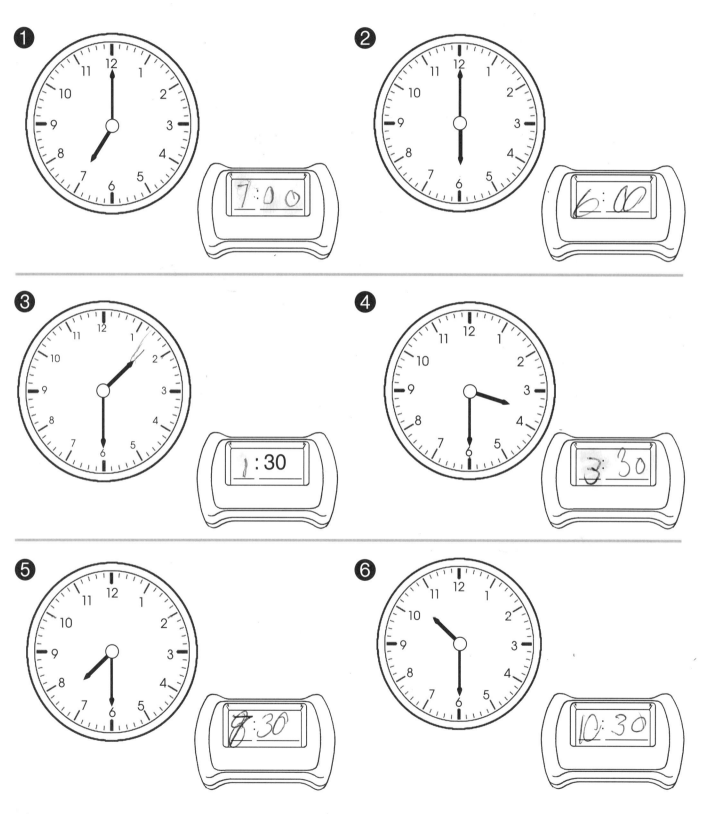

1. 7:00

2. 6:00

3. 1:30

4. 3:30

5. 7:30

6. 10:30

☆ **Tell how you know when it is 1:30.**

Name _____

Solve.

1 What time does this clock say?

 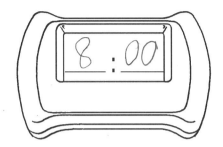

2 What time does this clock say?

 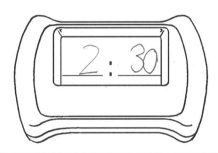

3 Circle the clock that shows 6:30.

4 Circle the clock that shows 3:30.

  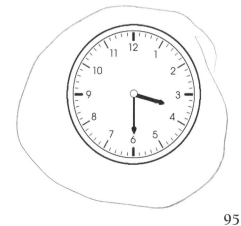

Unit 19
Interpret Data

Standard

Measurement and Data
Represent and interpret data.
1.MD.4 Organize, represent, and interpret data with up to three categories; ask and answer questions about the total number of data points, how many in each category, and how many more or less are in one category than in another.

Model the Skill

◆ Hand out two colors of counters (4 red and 2 yellow) and draw a 6 x 2 picture graph on the board titled "How Many Counters?"

How Many Counters?					
yellow					
red					

◆ **Say:** *This is called a picture graph. It shows information using pictures.* Read the title and point out the parts of the graph and explain their meanings.

◆ Instruct students to move the counters onto the graph. **Ask:** *Where will you put the yellow counters?* (in the first row) Tell students to always begin with the box next to the picture and that no boxes should be skipped. Repeat for the red counters.

◆ Explain that by looking at the graph, they can find information or data. **Ask:** *How many yellow counters are there?* (2) Tell students not to count the shaded counters at the head of each row.

◆ **Ask:** *Which has more?* (red) *A longer row means that that object has more than a shorter row.*

Assess the Skill

Use the following activity to pre-/post-assess students' understanding of the skill.

◆ **Say:** *Take a handful of 3 different color counters.*
Then draw a pictograph that shows the counters you picked.

Name _____

Place counters on the ones shown. Move them onto the picture graph. Record your work.

How Many Counters?					
yellow					
red					

❶ How many are there? ____3____

yellow

❷ Which one has more?   red   yellow

❸ Which one has less?   red   yellow

❹ How many more than ? ____2____

red   yellow

☆ **Write the number that shows how many red counters.**

Name _____

Use the graph to answer the questions.

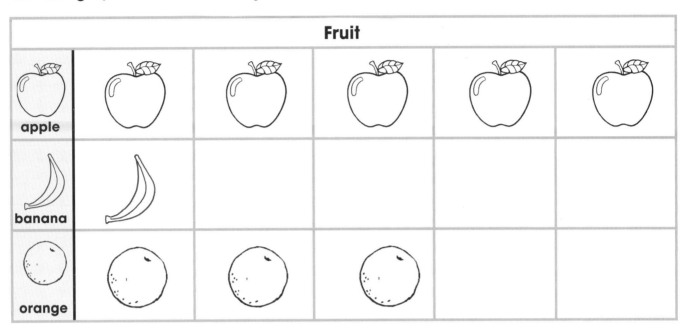

1 How many oranges are there? _____ 3 _____

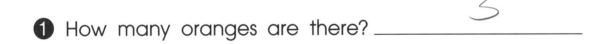

2 Which fruit has the least?

3 How many more apples are there than bananas? _____ 4 _____

4 How many fewer oranges are there than apples? _____ 2 _____

3

 Tell how you found the total number of oranges.

●●○ Unit 19 • Common Core Mathematics Grade 1 • ©2012 Newmark Learning, LLC

Use the graph to answer the questions.

Favorite Types of Travel						
train						
bus						
plane						

❶ How many buses are there ? _____ 3 _____

❷ Which type has the most votes?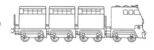

❸ How many fewer voted for trains than planes? _____ 4 _____

❹ How many votes were there in all? _____ 11 _____

  Tell how the pictograph helps you compare votes.

Name _____

Use the graph to answer the questions.

Types of Toys		
	⚪	
	⚪	
	⚪	
🪢	⚪	
🪢	⚪	
🪢	⚪	✶
🪢	⚪	✶
Jump ropes	**Balls**	**Jacks**

❶ Which toy has the most?

_____

❷ How many more jump ropes are there than jacks ? _____ 2 _____

_____

❸ How many more balls are there than jump ropes? _____ 3 _____

_____

❹ How many fewer jacks are there than balls? _____ 5 _____

Unit 20
Use Plane Shapes

Standard

Geometry
Reason with shapes and their attributes.
1.G.1 Distinguish between defining attributes (e.g., triangles are closed and three-sided) versus non-defining attributes (e.g., color, orientation, overall size); build and draw shapes to possess defining attributes.

Model the Skill

◆ Hand out pattern blocks.

◆ Draw a square on the board. **Ask:** *What is this shape?* (square) *How many sides does a square have?* (4) *How many corners does it have?* (4) Remind students that all sides are equal. Tell students that a square is a special type of rectangle because all the sides are equal.

◆ **Ask:** *Does it matter what color a shape is?* (no) *Does it matter if you turn the shape?* (no) Help students find all the squares and circle them. (Check students' work.)

◆ Assign students the appropriate practice page(s) to support their understanding of the skill. Discuss that shapes can be any size, can be any color, can be turned in any direction, and must have all sides touching. Review the difference between a plane two-dimensional shape and a solid three-dimensional shape.

Assess the Skill

Use the following activities to pre-/post-assess students' understanding of the skill.

◆ **Say:** *Use triangular pattern blocks to make a . . .*

• square

• rectangle

• larger triangle

Name _____

Draw a circle around all of the squares.

1

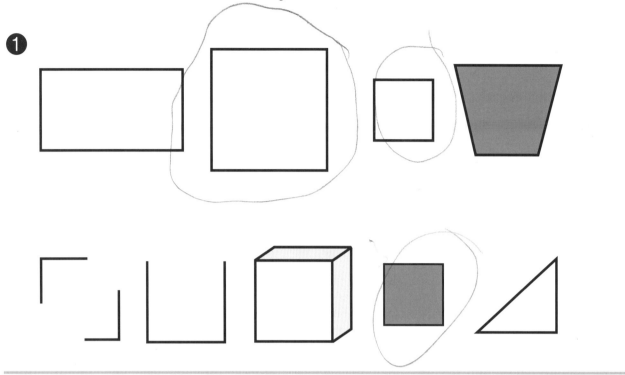

Circle all of the rectangles.

2

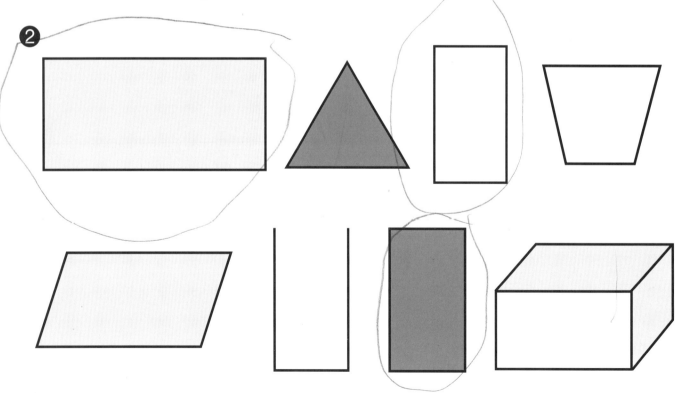

 Underline the triangles on this page.

●○○

Draw a circle around all of the triangles.

Circle all of the trapezoids.

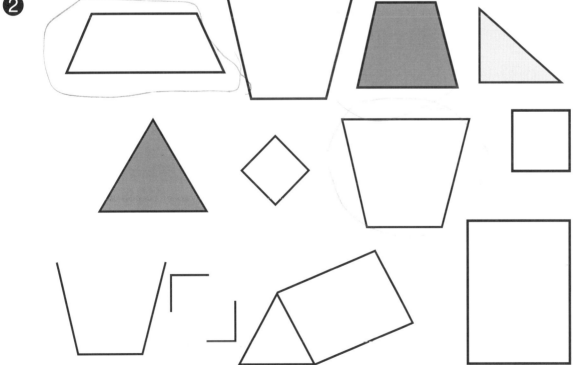

 Compare rectangles and trapezoids. How are they alike? How they are different?

Name _____

 Cut out the shapes. For each problem, build the shape. Trace the shape you made.

1 Make a rectangle.

2 Make a square.

3 Make a triangle.

4 Make a trapezoid.

 Tell how you used the triangles to make a square.

●●●

Name _____

Read each question. Then write the answer.

1 Draw a circle around the 2 shapes you would use to make a rectangle.

2 Draw a circle around the 2 shapes do you would use to make a square.

3 Draw a circle around the 3 shapes do you would use to make a trapezoid.

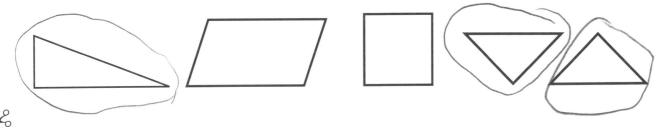

Cut out these shapes. Use them to make a square.

Unit 21
Use Solid Shapes

Geometry
Reason with shapes and their attributes.
1.G.2 Compose two-dimensional shapes (rectangles, squares, trapezoids, triangles, half-circles, and quarter-circles) or three-dimensional shapes (cubes, right rectangular prisms, right circular cones, and right circular cylinders) to create a composite shape, and compose new shapes from the composite shape.

Model the Skill

◆ Hand out cubes and rectangular prisms.

◆ **Say:** *Today we will work with solid shapes. Solid shapes are not flat like plane shapes. You can hold them.* Hold up a cube. **Ask:** *What is the name of this shape?* (cube) *How many sides or faces does a cube have?* (6) *How many corners does it have?* (8) Point out that all the sides are equal.

◆ Hold up a rectangular prism. **Ask:** *What is this shape?* (rectangular prism) *How many sides or faces does it have?* (6) *How many corners does it have?* (8) Discuss how it is similar to and different from a cube.

◆ Direct students to build a wall. **Ask:** *What shapes will you need for the bottom of the wall?* (cubes and rectangular prisms). Make sure students line them up in a row in the same order as shown. Have them follow each step, putting each row on top of the previous one.

◆ Assign students the appropriate practice page(s) to support their understanding of the skill.

Assess the Skill

Use the following activities to pre-/post-assess students' understanding of the skill.

Name _____

Use solid shapes. Build a building.

1 Place these shapes on the bottom.

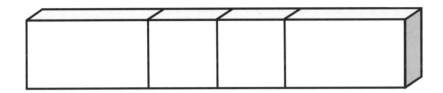

2 Then place these shapes on top of the others.

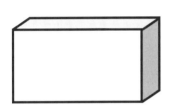  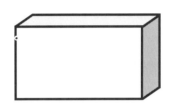

3 Next, place these shapes on top.

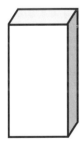 

4 Place these shapes on top of the 2 rectangular prisms .

 Circle the shapes you used 2 of to make the building.

Name _____

Use solid shapes. Build a castle.

1 Place these shapes on the bottom.

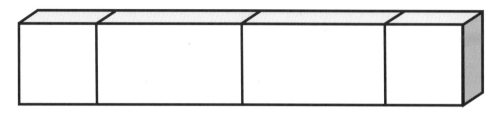

2 Then place these shapes on top of the others.

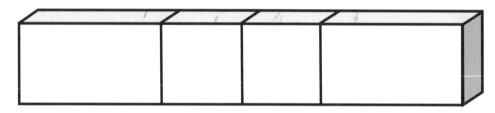

3 Next, place these shapes on top.

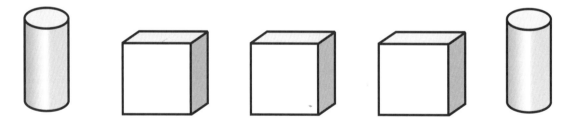

4 Place these shapes on top of the 2 .

cylinders

 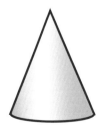

 Tell how cones and cylinders are alike and how they are different.

Use solid shapes to make a building. Draw your picture. Record your work.

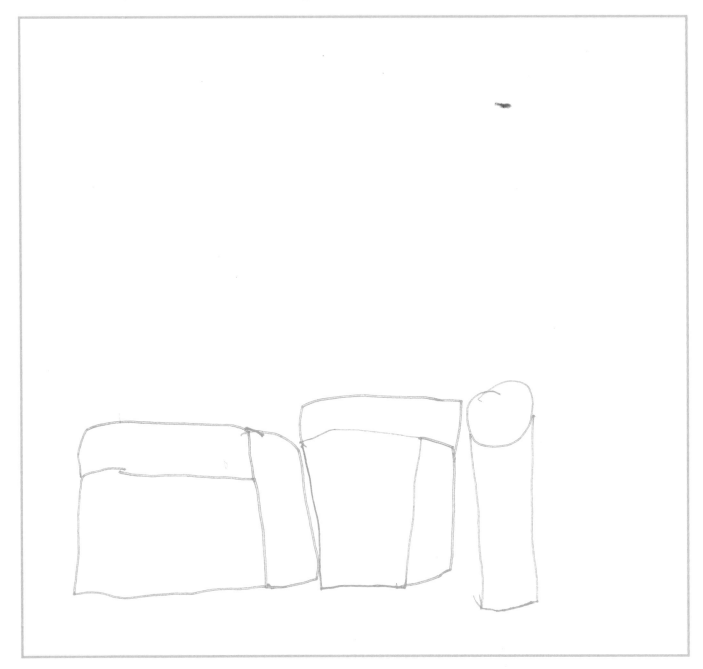

How many of each solid shape did you use? Write the number on the line.

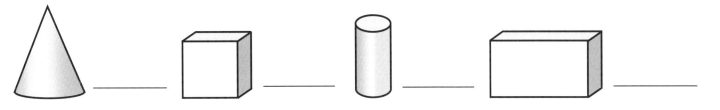

☆ **Tell how you built your building. What did you do first? What did you do last?**

Name _____

Build the building.

1 Place these shapes on the bottom:

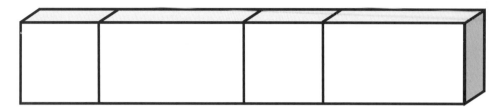

2 Then place these shapes on top of the others.

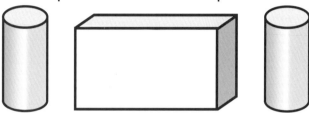

3 Next, place these shapes on top of the 2 .

cylinders

Write how many of each shape were used in this picture.

4 _____

 _____

 _____

 _____

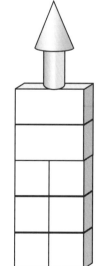

Unit 22
Parts of Shapes

Standard

Geometry
Reason with shapes and their attributes.
1.G.3 Partition circles and rectangles into two and four equal shares, describe the shares using the words halves, fourths, and quarters, and use the phrases half of, fourth of, and quarter of. Describe the whole as two of, or four of the shares. Understand for these examples that decomposing into more equal shares creates smaller shares.

Model the Skill

◆ Hand out blank pieces of paper.

◆ **Ask:** *Did you ever have one of something that you had to share with someone?* Discuss the need for equal shares. **Say:** *Pretend you want to share this piece of paper with a friend. Draw a line making 2 equal shares.* (Check students' drawings.)

◆ Introduce the word **half** to students. Discuss that there is more than 1 way to make two equal shares, or halves. **Say:** *Now you will draw a different line to make the next rectangle into two equal shares.* Check that students have drawn a different line than they drew for the first problem.

◆ Assign students the appropriate practice page(s) to support their understanding of the skill.

Assess the Skill

Use the following problems to pre-/post-assess students' understanding of the skill.

◆ Draw each shape. Then ask students to draw a line that divides each shape into two equal shares. Repeat with four equal shares.

Name _____

For each problem, draw a line to make two equal shares.

❶

❷

❸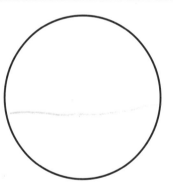

❹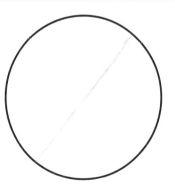

 Draw another way to make 2 equal shares of a rectangle.

●○○

Name _____

For each problem, draw lines to make four equal shares.

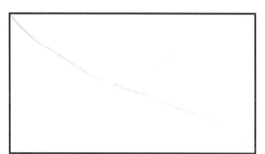

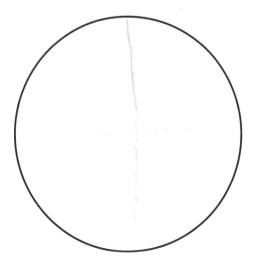

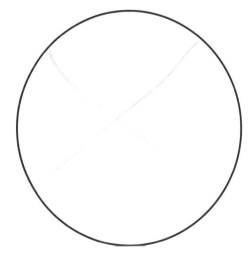

 Tell how you know the shares are equal.

Name _____

For each problem, write how many equal shares make a whole.

1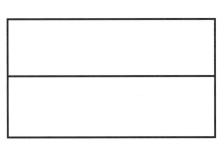

_____

2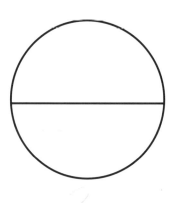

_____

3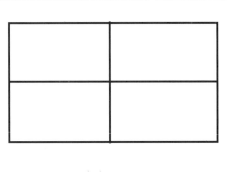

_____

4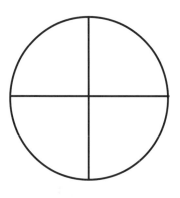

_____

5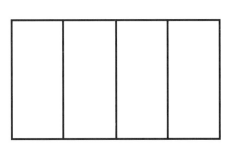

_____

6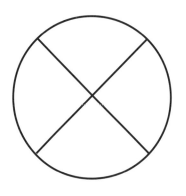

_____

☆ **Tell how you know the shares are equal in Problems 3 and 5.**

Solve.

1 Circle the items with one-half of the shape shaded.

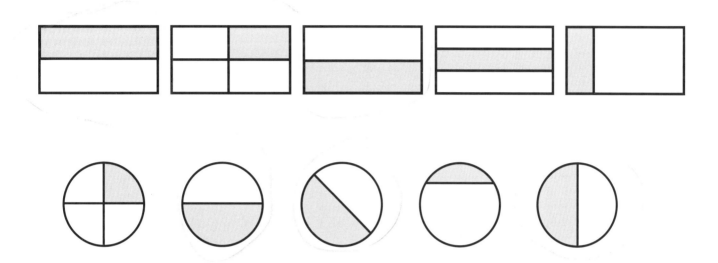

---

2 Circle the items with one-fourth or one-quarter of the shape shaded.

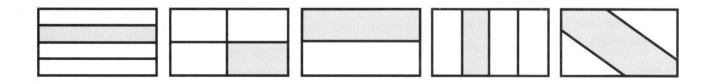

Name _____

Solve. Show your work.

❶ 4 + 5 = _9_

❷ 6 + 8 = _14_

❸ 7 + 2 = _9_

❹ 12 + 3 = 15

❺ 14 + 3 = 17

❻ 19 + 2 = 21

❼ 7 + 2 = 9

❽ 6 + 6 = 12

Name _____

Add to solve each problem. Show your work.

❶ $2 + 3 = \underline{5}$ ❷ $6 + 3 = \underline{9}$

❸ $4 + 8 = \underline{12}$ ❹ $8 + 5 = \underline{13}$

❺ $7 + 6 = \underline{13}$ ❻ $6 + 5 = \underline{11}$

❼ $9 + 8 = \underline{17}$ ❽ $4 + 7 = \underline{11}$

Name _____

Solve. Show your work.

1

$6 + 3 = \underline{9}$ $9 - 3 = \underline{6}$ $9 - 6 = \underline{3}$

2

$12 - 5 = \underline{7}$ $12 - 7 = \underline{5}$ $7 + 5 = \underline{12}$

3

$14 - 8 = \underline{6}$ $14 - 6 = \underline{8}$ $6 + 8 = \underline{4}$

4

$12 - 4 = \underline{8}$ $8 + 4 = \underline{12}$ $12 - 8 = \underline{4}$

Fill in the missing number.

1 $6 + 4 = \underline{10}$

2 $5 + 7 = \underline{12}$

3 $12 - \underline{6} = 6$

4 $13 - \underline{5} = 8$

5 $\underline{4} + 9 = 13$

6 $\underline{6} + 8 = 14$

7 $8 = 17 - \underline{9}$

8 $6 = 13 - \underline{7}$

Name _____

Fill in the missing numbers.

1

50	51	52	53	54	55

2

61	62	63	64	65	66

3

73	74	75	76	77	78

4

96	97	98	99	100	101

5

103	104	105	106	107	108

6

115	116	117	118	119	120

Common Core Mathematics Grade 1 • ©2012 Newmark Learning, LLC

Add to solve each problem. Show your work.

❶ 23   20   tens
          9   ones
         ____

❷ 47   50   tens
         ____   ones
         ____

❸ 76   ____ tens
         ____ ones
         ____

❹ 32   ____ tens
         ____ ones
         ____

❺ 91   ____ tens
         ____ ones
         ____

❻ 65   ____ tens
         ____ ones
         ____

❼ 44   ____ tens
         ____ ones
         ____

❽ 89   ____ tens
         ____ ones
         ____

Name _____

Compare the numbers. Write <, >, or =.

1 37  34

2 71  70

---

3 53 58

4 21  21

---

5 38 ◯ 41

6 87 78

---

7 61 ◯ 59

8 93 ◯ 98

Name _____

Compare the numbers. Write <, >, or =.

❶ 51 ◯ 52

❷ 60 ◯ 79

❸ 35 ◯ 41

❹ 19 ◯ 23

❺ 20 ◯ 28

❻ 40 ◯ 39

❼ 63 ◯ 58

❽ 82 ◯ 28

Name _____

Solve each problem. Show your work.

❶ $14 + 5 =$ ___   ❷ $26 + 4 =$ ___

❸ $37 + 2 =$ ___   ❹ $45 + 3 =$ ___

❺ $4 + 23 =$ ___   ❻ $29 + 2 =$ ___

❼ $7 +$ ___ $= 79$ ❽ ___ $- 6 = 42$

Common Core Mathematics Grade 1 • ©2012 Newmark Learning, LLC

Add to solve each problem. Show your work.

❶ $45 + 10 =$ ___   ❷ $16 + 10 =$ ___

❸ $27 + 10 =$ ___   ❹ $59 + 10 =$ ___

❺ $11 + 10 =$ ___   ❻ $72 + 10 =$ ___

❼ $57 +$ ___ $= 67$ ❽ ___ $+ 10 = 12$

Name Adline

Solve each problem. Show your work.

❶ $40 + 10 = \underline{50}$

❷ $27 - 10 = \underline{\hspace{2cm}}$

❸ $84 + 10 = \underline{\hspace{2cm}}$

❹ $81 - 10 = \underline{\hspace{2cm}}$

❺ $39 + 10 = \underline{\hspace{2cm}}$

❻ $73 - 10 = \underline{\hspace{2cm}}$

❼ $68 + 10 = \underline{\hspace{2cm}}$

❽ $95 - 10 = \underline{\hspace{2cm}}$

Solve each problem. Show your work.

❶ $74 + 20 = \underline{}$ ❷ $16 + 40 = \underline{}$

❸ $46 - 30 = \underline{}$ ❹ $12 - 10 = \underline{}$

❺ $24 + 60 = \underline{}$ ❻ $67 - 20 = \underline{}$

❼ $79 + \underline{} = 99$ ❽ $\underline{} - 60 = 22$

Name _____

Solve each problem. Show your work.

❶ $31 + 50 =$ ___   **❷** $78 - 60 =$ ___

❸ $75 + 20 =$ ___   **❹** $72 - 20 =$ ___

❺ $93 - 30 =$ ___   **❻** $29 - 20 =$ ___

❼ $50 +$ ___ $= 79$ **❽** ___ $- 30 = 17$

Subtract to solve each problem. Show your work.

❶ $40 - 10 =$ _____

❷ $27 - 20 =$ _____

❸ $84 - 40 =$ _____

❹ $81 - 70 =$ _____

❺ $79 - 40 =$ _____

❻ $53 - 50 =$ _____

❼ $35 - 20 =$ _____

❽ $96 - 50 =$ _____

Traditional Hundreds Chart

1	2	3	4	5	6	7	8	9	10
11	12	13	14	15	16	17	18	19	20
21	22	23	24	25	26	27	28	29	30
31	32	33	34	35	36	37	38	39	40
41	42	43	44	45	46	47	48	49	50
51	52	53	54	55	56	57	58	59	60
61	62	63	64	65	66	67	68	69	70
71	72	73	74	75	76	77	78	79	80
81	82	83	84	85	86	87	88	89	90
91	92	93	94	95	96	97	98	99	100

Common Core Mathematics Grade 1 • ©2012 Newmark Learning, LLC

Five-Frame

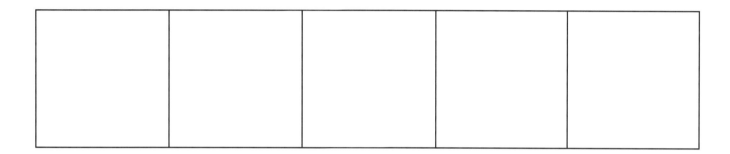

Ten-Frame

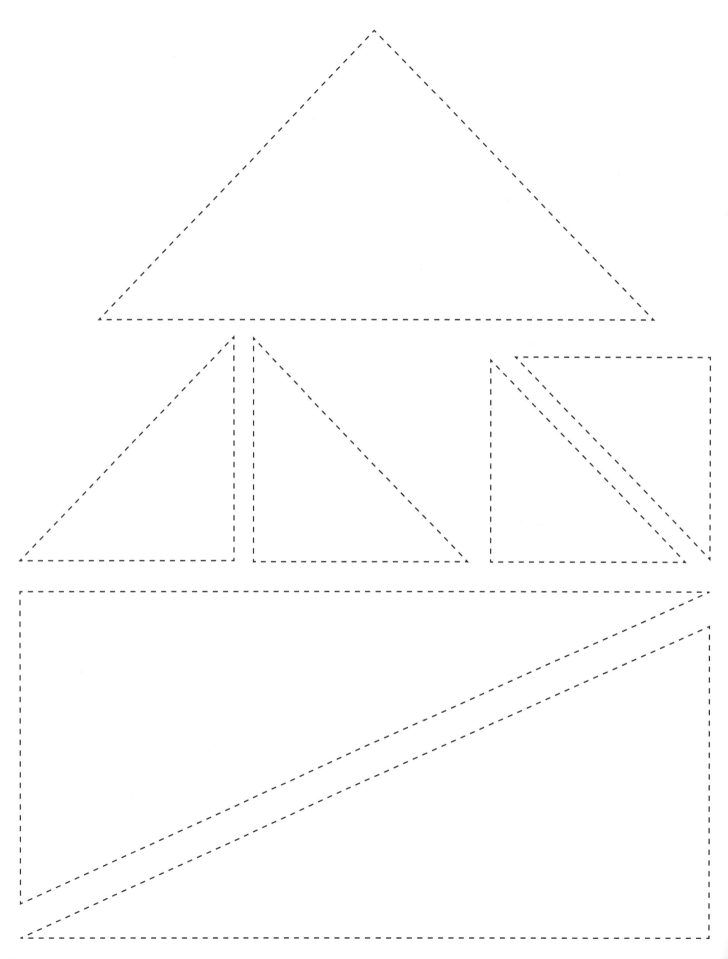

Common Core Mathematics Grade 1 • ©2012 Newmark Learning, LLC

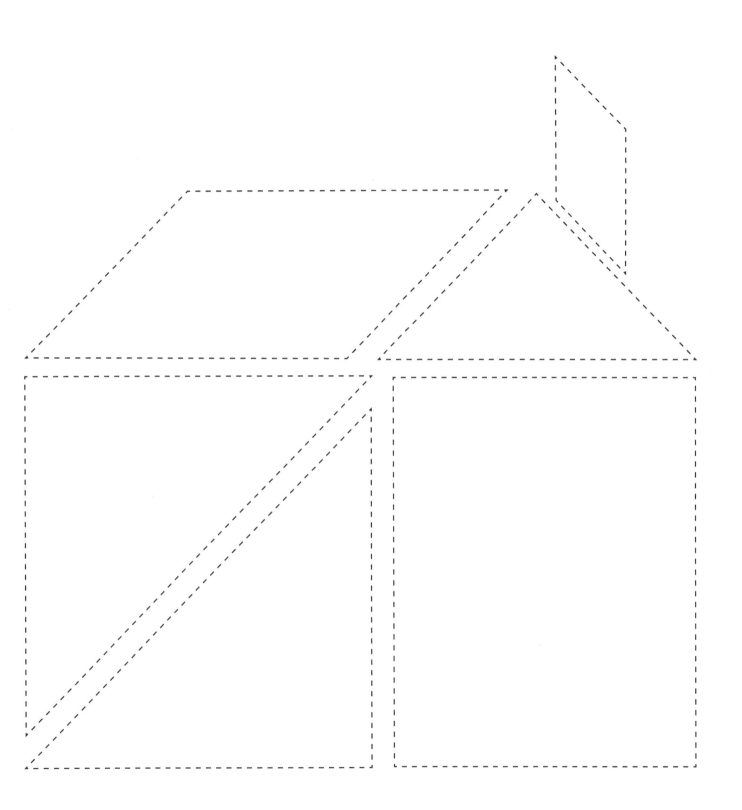

Name _____

Answer Key • Units 1–5

Unit 1 (p. 7)
•
1. 9 turtles
2. 8 birds
3. 8 ducks

Unit 1 (p. 8)
••
1. 12 cars
2. 8 crayons
3. 4 muffins

Unit 1 (p. 9)
•••
1. 14 dolls
2. 9 clips
3. 5 rolls
4. 18 balloons

Unit 1 (p. 10)
Word Problems
1. 11 ducks
2. 5 pencils
3. 8 marbles
4. 6 frogs

Unit 2 (p. 12)
•
1. 6 bananas
2. 8 cups
3. 11 trucks
4. 5 corn muffins

Unit 2 (p. 13)
••
1. 14 crayons
2. 8 buses
3. 7 swings
4. 3 + 3 = 6, 2 + 4= 6, 1 + 5 = 6, or 6 + 0= 6

Unit 2 (p. 14)
•••
1. 5 horses
2. 12 pigs
Possible answers:
3. 4 + 4 = 8   5 + 3= 8
4. 5 + 5 = 10 6 + 4= 10

Unit 2 (p. 15)
Word Problems
1. 12 plants 2. 2 fish
Possible answers:
3. 4 + 3 = 7, 5 + 2= 7
4. 3 + 3 = 6   4 + 2= 6

Unit 3 (p. 17)
•
1. 3 more stickers
2. 3 more pencils
3. 7 more pens

Unit 3 (p. 18)
••
1. 5 crayons
2. 5 fewer leaves
3. 8 fewer buttons
4. 9 fewer flowers

Unit 3 (p. 19)
•••
1. 7 apples
2. 14 marbles
3. 6 fewer goldfish
4. 10 fewer shells

Unit 3 (p. 20)
Word Problems
1. 3 fewer pears
2. 2 more books
3. 9 stamps
4. 4 balloons

Unit 4 (p. 22)
•
1. 9 flowers
2. 12 fish
3. 16 children

Unit 4 (p. 23)
••
1. 13 jars
2. 11 blocks
3. 9 cars
4. 13 cupcakes

Unit 4 (p. 24)
•••
1. 10 cards
2. 16 pencils
3. 12 buttons
4. 11 leaves

Unit 4 (p. 25)
Word Problems
1. 9 cars
2. 10 leaves
3. 15 shirts
4. 15 pens

Unit 5 (p. 27)
•
1. 6
2. 10
3. 11

Unit 5 (p. 28)
••
Check students' work.
1. 8
2. 10
3. 18
4. 13

Unit 5 (p. 29)
•••
1. 12
2. 13
3. 16
4. 16

Unit 5 (p. 30)
Word Problems
1. 1st
2. 1st
3. 2nd
4. 2nd

Common Core Mathematics Grade 1 • ©2012 Newmark Learning, LLC

Answer Key • Units 6–10

Unit 6 (p. 32)
•
1. 7
2. 8
3. 6
4. 10

Unit 6 (p. 33)
••
1. 17
2. 19
3. 16
4. 20
5. 14
6. 16

Unit 6 (p. 34)
•••
1. 12
2. 16
3. 14
4. 11
5. 11
6. 13

Unit 6 (p. 35)
Word Problems
1. 2nd
2. 1st
3. 1st
4. 2nd

Unit 7 (p. 37)
•
1. 2
2. 2
3. 6
4. 7

Unit 7 (p. 38)
••
1. 19
2. 12
3. 13
4. 16
5. 14
6. 11

Unit 7 (p. 39)
•••
Answers may vary.
1. $6 + 1 = 7$ $7 - 1 = 6$
2. $3 + 5 = 8$ $8 - 3 = 5$
3. $7 + 3 = 10$ $10 - 3 = 7$
4. $6 + 5 = 11$ $11 - 5 = 6$
5. $7 + 4 = 11$ $11 - 7 = 4$
6. $8 + 9 = 17$ $17 - 9 = 8$

Unit 7 (p. 40)
Word Problems
1. 7
2. 8
3. 9
4. 7

Unit 8 (p. 42)
•
1. 3
2. 9
3. 4
4. 8

Unit 8 (p. 43)
••
1. 11   2. 15
3. 10   4. 10
5. 4   6. 1

Unit 8 (p. 44)
•••
1. 7   2. 2
3. 3   4. 4
5. 8   6. 8
7. 7   8. 3

Unit 8 (p. 45)
Word Problems
1. 9   2. 3
3. 6   4. 7

Unit 9 (p. 47)
•
1. 14; 16
2. 25, 26; 29
3. 81, 82; 84, 85
4. 99; 102; 103

Unit 9 (p. 48)
••
1. 72; 74, 75
2. 63, 64; 66
3. 88, 89, 90; 92
4. 96, 97, 98; 100
5. 106, 107, 108; 110
6. 114, 115, 116, 117

Unit 9 (p. 49)
•••
1. 1st
2. 2nd
3. 2nd
4. 2nd
5. 1st
6. 2nd

Unit 9 (p. 50)
Word Problems
1. 85; 87
2. 47, 48; 50, 51
3. 116, 117, 118; 120
4. 78

Unit 10 (p. 52)
•
1. 11
2. 12
3. 13
4. 14

Unit 10 (p. 53)
••
1. 5 ones; 15
2. 6 ones ;16
3. 7 ones ;17
4. 8 ones ;18
5. 7 ones ;17

Unit 10 (p. 54)
•••
1. 20
2. 50
3. 35
4. 61
5. 46
6. 74

Unit 10 (p. 55)
Word Problems
1. 1   2. 7
3. 4   4. 0
5. 5; 2; 52
6. 8; 6; 86
7. 6   8. 0

Name _____

Answer Key • Units 11–15

Unit 11 (p. 57)
●
1. 23 < 58
2. 71 = 71
3. 49 < 74
4. 86 > 82

Unit 11 (p. 58)
●●
1. 67 < 92
2. 26 = 26
3. 58 > 54
4. 31 > 13

Unit 11 (p. 59)
●●●
1. 42 < 48 **2.** 39 > 14
3. 69 = 69 **4.** 40 < 73
5. 74 < 78 **6.** 56 = 56

Unit 11 (p. 60)
Word Problems
1–3:
Check students' work.
Answers 1-3 may vary.
4. 98

Unit 12 (p. 62)
●
1. 17
2. 38
3. 68

Unit 12 (p. 63)
●●
1. 42
2. 51
3. 62
4. 71

Unit 12 (p. 64)
●●●
1. 19
2. 36
3. 69
4. 58
5. 90
6. 25

Unit 12 (p. 65)
Word Problems
1. 34
2. 44
3. 46
4. 69
5. 90
6. 92

Unit 13 (p. 67)
●
1. 30
2. 23
3. 55
4. 66

Unit 13 (p. 68)
●●
1. 60
2. 46
3. 34
4. 80

Unit 13 (p. 69)
●●●
1. 40 **2.** 60
3. 51 **4.** 93
5. 85 **6.** 6

Unit 13 (p. 70)
Word Problems
1. 77
2. 34
3. 48
4. 8

Unit 14 (p. 72)
●
1. 20
2. 60
3. 72
4. 87

Unit 14 (p. 73)
●●
1. 50
2. 75
3. 89
4. 94

Unit 14 (p. 74)
●●●
1. 50 **2.** 90
3. 40 **4.** 71
5. 95 **6.** 59

Unit 14 (p. 75)
Word Problems
1. 83 **2.** 86
3. 80 **4.** 63
5. 75 **6.** 77

Unit 15 (p. 77)
●
1. 10
2. 20
3. 31
4. 46

Unit 15 (p. 78)
●●
1. 30
2. 50
3. 61
4. 14

Unit 15 (p. 79)
●●●
1. 10 **2.** 20
3. 54 **4.** 42
5. 47 **6.** 6

Unit 15 (p. 80)
Word Problems
1. 32 **2.** 17
3. 68 **4.** 23
5. 7 **6.** 19

Answer Key • Units 16–20

Unit 16 (p. 82)
•
1. circle; underline
2. underline; circle
3. circle; underline

Unit 16 (p. 83)
••
1. 2; 3; 1
2. 3; 1; 2
3. 2; 3; 1
4. 3; 2; 1

Unit 16 (p. 84)
•••
1. 1; 3; 2
2. 2; 1; 3
3. 1; 3; 2
4. 3; 1; 2

Unit 16 (p. 85)
Word Problems
Answers may vary.

Unit 17 (p. 87)
•
1. 3
2. 2
3. 5
4. 4

Unit 17 (p. 88)
••
1. 2
2. 3
3. 2
4. 5

Unit 17 (p. 89)
•••
1. 1
2. 4
3. 2
4. 3

Unit 17 (p. 90)
Word Problems
1. 2
2. 4
3. 5

Unit 18 (p. 92)
•
1. 1:00
2. 4:30
3. 3:30
4. 11:00

Unit 18 (p. 93)
••
1. 2:00
2. 5:00
3. 8:30
4. 11:30

Unit 18 (p. 94)
•••
1. 7:00   2. 6:00
3. 1:30   4. 3:30
5. 7:30   6. 10:30

Unit 18 (p. 95)
1. 8:00
2. 2:30
3. 2nd
4. 3rd

Unit 19 (p. 97)
•
1. 3
2. red
3. yellow
4. 2

Unit 19 (p. 98)
••
1. 3
2. banana
3. 4
4. 2

Unit 19 (p. 99)
•••
1. 3
2. plane
3. 4
4. 11

Unit 19 (p. 100)
Interpret Data Practice
1. balls
2. 2
3. 3
4. 5

Unit 20 (p. 102)
•

Check students' work.

Unit 20 (p. 103)
••

Check students' work.

Unit 20 (p. 104)
•••

Check students' work.

Unit 20 (p. 105)
Word Problems

Check students' work.

Name _____

Answer Key • Units 21–22

Unit 21 (p. 107)
•

Check students' work.

Unit 21 (p. 108)
••

Check students' work.

Unit 21 (p. 109)
•••

Check students' work.

Unit 21 (p. 110)
Practice Using Solid Shapes

Check students' work.

Unit 22 (p. 112)
•

Check students' work.

Unit 22 (p. 113)
••

Check students' work.

Unit 22 (p. 114)
•••

1. 2 **2.** 2
3. 4 **4.** 4
5. 4 **6.** 4

Unit 22 (p. 115)
Word Problems

Check students' work.

Answer Key • Fluency Practice

p. 116

1. 9   2. 14
3. 9   4. 15
5. 17   6. 21
7. 2   8. 6

p. 117

1. 5   2. 9
3. 12   4. 13
5. 13   6. 11
7. 17   8. 11

p. 118

1. 9 ; 6 ; 3
2. 7; 5; 12
3. 6 ; 8 ; 14
4. 8 ; 12 ; 4

p. 119

1. 10   2. 12
3. 6   4. 5
5. 4   6. 6
7. 9   8. 7

p. 120

1. 51; 54, 55
2. 63, 64; 66
3. 74, 75, 76; 78
4. 97, 98, 99; 101
5. 104, 105, 106; 108
6. 116, 117; 119, 120

p. 121

1. 2 tens; 3 ones
2. 4 tens; 7 ones
3. 7 tens; 6 ones
4. 3 tens; 2 ones
5. 9 tens; 1 ones
6. 6 tens; 5 ones
7. 4 tens; 4 ones
8. 8 tens; 9 ones

p. 122

1. >   2. >
3. <   4. =
5. <   6. >
7. >   8. <

p. 123

1. <   2. <
3. <   4. <
5. <   6. >
7. >   8. >

p. 124

1. 19   2. 30
3. 39   4. 48
5. 27   6. 31
7. 72   8. 48

p. 125

1. 55   2. 26
3. 37   4. 69
5. 21   6. 82
7. 10   8. 2

p. 126

1. 50
2. 17
3. 94
4. 71
5. 49
6. 63
7. 78
8. 85

p. 127

1. 94   2. 56
3. 16   4. 2
5. 84   6. 47
7. 20   8. 82

p. 128

1. 81   2. 18
3. 95   4. 52
5. 63   6. 9
7. 29   8. 47

p. 129

1. 30   2. 7
3. 44   4. 11
5. 39   6. 3
7. 15   8. 46

Notes